THE MANAGER'S POCKET GUIDE TO
Emotional Intelligence

From Management to Leadership

By Emily A. Sterrett, Ph.D.

HRD PRESS
Amherst, Massachusetts

Published by:
HRD Press
22 Amherst Road
Amherst, MA 01002
1-800-822-2801
  (U.S. and Canada)
1-413-253-3490 (Fax)
http://www.hrdpress.com

Printed in Canada

ISBN 0-87425-597-6

Production services by Clark Riley
Cover design by Eileen Klockars
Editorial services by Robie Grant

TABLE OF CONTENTS

FOREWORD

A number of books have been written in the last few years about Emotional Intelligence, or EQ — the characteristics other than "brainpower" that successful leaders possess. Many of these books are quite good and well worth reading but are written for researchers, or professionals such as social workers or counselors for use in therapy. Few offer practical suggestions as to how we can develop or expand our own EQ and that of those who work for us. The average manager needs an introduction to this important concept without having to wade through information that might not be directly relevant to his or her organization and its specific challenges.

This book is written to introduce managers to the concept of Emotional Intelligence — managers who are young or not-so-young, experienced or novice, supervisors or CEOs. Emotional Intelligence refers to the intelligence that all successful people bring to their jobs that does not come under the category of "book smarts" or ability to reason. It is a large part of what makes people successful in leadership positions and in all of life.

Emotional Intelligence or EQ is not a simple repackaging of the "soft skills" we so often hear about in business. It is based on research. Good managers have known for years that communicating effectively, treating people well, and modeling appropriate behavior themselves makes good business sense. Now we have the proof: research linking emotions and social skills on one hand and facts and figures on the other.

There's no need to throw away cognitive (thinking) processes, but by themselves these are not enough for success in the organization. The plain truth is we need both rational data and emotional data in our lives if we are to be successful in business, in the organization, and in life. This book shows you how to develop hidden capabilities and find the right balance between the rational and the emotional. *You can have both.*

Emotional Intelligence as a concept covers a lot of territory, so condensing it into a book that can be read in just a few hours was a daunting task. But you will find this "primer" on EQ easy to follow and, more important, filled with ideas an how to put Emotional Intelligence to wise use in your own life. The key is *wanting* to do it and making a commitment to *work on it* one step at a time. Where will you be professionally in five years? When that time rolls around, why not be more of the person or the leader you want to be! If your career and other relationships are not what you'd like them to be, if you feel stuck, if you often feel overwhelmed and anxious or discouraged and lethargic, **you need the information in this book**.

Use this Pocket Guide as a workbook — your personal guide to greater productivity and satisfaction. You can even read it with your staff and discuss it as a team. Each individual will find particular areas in which to begin his or her own developmental plan to move ahead and reach his or her leadership potential, but making changes will take much longer than a quick read through the book. It is a process, and you *are* worth it, so let's get started!

CHAPTER 1

Defining Emotional Intelligence (EQ)

Jack walked into the office where three of his sales managers were reviewing the latest sales figures. So engrossed were they in discussing the disappointing results and what might be causing the sudden downturn in business, they did not hear him approach. Jack cleared his throat rather loudly, interrupting an obviously important and spirited discussion about work. "Kelly," he said firmly, "I need to see you about that Allied account. We need to get some information to corporate." He turned on his heels, leaving Kelly to wrinkle up her nose and explain to her colleagues that she would have to get back to them about continuing this analysis. She quickly followed Jack to his office.

Assuming that the information corporate needed did not represent a crisis, how would you assess Jack's handling of this situation? What effect did his approach have on Kelly and her colleagues?

Jack, like too many managers, used the "boss" technique to get what he wanted done. He demonstrated poor social skills and possibly did long-term damage to goodwill by first assuming that the obviously work-related discussion was not particularly important, and then by barging in on it. Kelly and her colleagues would have been much more interested in complying with Jack's request had he:

1) waited until there was a good stopping point in their conversation and they acknowledged his presence;

2) greeted them with a few pleasant words;

3) asked what they were discussing and appeared interested in hearing about it (after all, he needs to know about the sales figures, too);

4) explained what he needed and then asked for Kelly's input on when and how she could comply with his request for information from corporate;

5) exchanged pleasant conversation as he and Kelly walked to his office to work on the request.

This could indeed have been a crisis, but when the manager or the organization is always operating in crisis mode, there are usually management problems. It's probably safe to conclude that Jack's behavior in this situation is an example of low "Emotional Intelligence."

Emotional Intelligence: A Definition

We are all familiar with the term *intelligence quotient*, or IQ, but few managers in today's workplaces understand much about **Emotional** Intelligence — what is now being called "**EQ**." Managers know a great deal about the products or services that their organizations deliver to customers, and they are becoming more knowledgeable about the technology that puts their organizations into the marketplace of ideas. When it comes to issues involving individuals or groups, however, many tend to fall short. Emotions and social skills don't appear to be as important to success in our jobs as facts and figures and processes.

Just what is Emotional Intelligence anyway? Often called EQ (Emotional-Intelligence quotient), Emotional Intelligence refers to the array of personal-management and social skills that allows one to succeed in the workplace and life in general. EQ encompasses intuition, character, integrity, and motivation. It also includes good communication and relationship skills.

But *emotions* in the workplace? Surely we want to keep emotions out of the organization! The business world, after all, moves on facts and figures — or so we think. But new evidence makes a pretty compelling case that poor emotional and social skills derail more careers than lack of technical expertise or even general intelligence — what we think of as IQ.

nterestingly, very little research has been done on the science of emotions in the past. In the last decade or so, the scientific and even business literature has been filled with new evidence explaining the neurophysiology and biochemistry of emotions and their roles in our professional and personal lives. Case studies of leaders and other successful people have added additional evidence to support the vital role of emotions in decision-making, leadership, and success in life. New research on the subject will teach us even more.

Think about your own experiences for a moment. Have you ever had a very strong "gut reaction" to a certain person or situation? Have you ever walked into a room and sensed that something was wrong, or taken a chance on something you just knew was the right thing, even though the "facts" said otherwise? Perhaps you weren't able to explain exactly why you reacted the way you did, but the sensation was powerful. This was the voice of your *intuition* — the gut feeling you had stemming from past emotional experiences stored in your brain. This "knowing" is inside us all, but many of us have been trained to ignore it in favor of rationality and logic.

Balancing Emotional and Intellectual Intelligences

When managers think of emotions, they often focus on overreactions that they have witnessed in the workplace — conflict, hurt feelings, or even their own embarrassing moments. Letting emotions overpower our intellect is *not* what we mean by Emotional Intelligence; in fact, quite the opposite is true: out-of-control emotions are not what we want, at work or elsewhere.

On the other hand, listening only to our rational, factual side is not Emotional Intelligence, either. Feelings, instincts, and intuitions gained through experience are vital sources of information about the world around us. We operate with only half the information we need to make valid decisions when we try to use only rational, cognitively derived data. This approach does not lead to overall success within any organization or to a satisfying personal life.

3

Psychologists quantify the rational thinking part of our brains; they call it "intelligence quotient," or IQ. Psychologists and educators do not agree on exactly how to measure it nor what the numbers really mean. Nonetheless, we have some widely used and accepted measures of intelligence: An IQ of 120 tells us something about a person's general ability, as does an IQ of 85. We have known for decades, however, that intelligence does not correlate highly with success on the job. In other words, being highly intelligent and using your cognitive skills do not guarantee success.

> ➤ **True Emotional Intelligence is being able to appropriately call upon information from the emotional center of the brain, and balance that with information from the rational center of the brain.**

Based on a number of recent studies, experts now believe that IQ, or general intelligence, contributes no more than 25% to one's overall success. Sure, it helps to be born with brainpower and even to develop it, but this is not enough for success in life or success in management. Some may advance the idea that having expertise in a certain field determines success; developing strong technical competency or specific intelligence in your chosen field can indeed be a necessary step for initial entry into the field, yet competency fails to add much to the success equation. Most experts believe it contributes only 10–20% to success.

So, if it's not just IQ and it's not just technical expertise, what else makes up the remainder of the formula for success — that remaining 55–65%? Case studies and longitudinal studies by highly regarded leaders give us a clue: Opportunity or serendipity adds a few percentage points, but many well-respected leaders create their own opportunities. They are able to do so because *they rank high on all dimensions of Emotional Intelligence.*

It is EQ that allows us to express preferences in decision-making, passionately pursue a goal, control our temper, and offer persuasive arguments for or against an idea. EQ explains why we like certain people better than others, and helps us get along with the ones we don't. It is EQ that helps us establish relationships and become politically savvy in the office, and it is what keeps us going in difficult times. If you think business is or *should* be based only on rational skills, the newest research would urge you to rethink this notion: Emotional Intelligence is the most fundamental dimension of leadership today and in the foreseeable future, and the higher we aspire to or rise in leadership positions, the more important it becomes.

Toward a Model of EQ

Emotional Intelligence, because of its "people-focus," is based on sound competency in two major dimensions: Self and Social. The high-EQ person must have *knowledge* and a *positive attitude*, and *behave skillfully* in the Self and Social dimensions.

Emotional Intelligence has been broken down into six areas, defined as follows:

SELF Dimension of Emotional Intelligence
Our Emotional Intelligence comes, in part, from our understanding and acceptance of ourselves in three areas:

1. Knowledge = **Self-Awareness**:
   Accurately knowing our own feelings, preferences, goals, and values; sensing how others feel about us, and using that information to guide our behavior.

2. Attitude = **Self-Confidence**:
   A "can-do" attitude, a belief in ourselves; overcoming self-doubt and taking reasonable risk; being assertive and not aggressive; being goal-directed; admitting mistakes and moving on.

3. Behavior = **Self-Control**:
   Dealing well with stress; controlling emotional moods or outbursts without overcontrol; being adaptable; balancing rational and emotional considerations.

> *SOCIAL Dimension of Emotional Intelligence*
> The other three facets of Emotional Intelligence have to do with the experience and interactions with others — our social relationships:

4. Knowledge = **Empathy**:
   Easily reading and understanding others; having empathy; listening well; reading non-verbal cues.

5. Attitude = **Motivation**:
   Taking initiative; having a positive outlook; being creative; inspiring others; doing things we believe in and are committed to.

6. Behavior = **Social Competency**:
   Finding common ground to establish rapport and minimize conflict; persuading and influencing others; being likable and having positive relationships; having integrity.

The six facets in Emotional Intelligence are illustrated in the model, which we refer to as the K-A-B Model (see p. 7).

There is an overlap between the Self and Social dimensions (we get some of our "self" information, and our attitude, from "social" relationships). Our knowledge, attitude, and behavior also intermingle, which is why the lines in the model are broken lines to show that the boundaries between the facets are fluid.

The rest of this Pocket Guide will introduce you to the science behind what we are now calling **Emotional Intelligence** and help you assess where your EQ needs bolstering. In it, we will explain the value of emotions at work, and provide you with specific techniques to improve your own EQ. *The Manager's Pocket Guide to Emotional Intelligence* will help you grow as a person and as a professional, and help you become more successful and more satisfied with your life and work.

Self Dimension of Emotional Intelligence

Knowledge: **Self-Awareness**
Attitude: **Self-Confidence**
Behavior: **Self-Control**

Attitude
Self-Confidence

**SELF
DIMENSION**

Knowledge
Self-Awareness

Behavior
Self-Control

Behavior
Social Competency

Knowledge
Empathy

**SOCIAL
DIMENSION**

Attitude
Motivation

Social Dimension of Emotional Intelligence

Knowledge: **Empathy**
Attitude: **Motivation**
Behavior: **Social Competency**

K-A-B Model of Emotional Intelligence

Improving Your EQ

Your EQ can continue to increase over your lifetime, and can even be improved in *every* arena of your life. In fact, life itself is the laboratory where we build greater EQ. You can work on your Emotional Intelligence when you are alone, or when you are with your employees, co-workers, family, friends, neighbors, or acquaintances. It will take 3–6 months to make any substantial improvement in Emotional Intelligence, but the payoff is worth it if you answer yes to any of these questions:

Do you want to be more in control at work or at home?

Would you like to be able to deal more effectively with personal stress?

Would you like to have a wider circle of influence?

Do you want to commit to and move ahead with your goals?

Would you like people around you to be more productive?

Do you long to take risks and overcome your fear of change?

Would you like to develop a more positive and hopeful attitude?

And, finally, do you want to live a more satisfying and successful life?

We can't really separate the rational from the emotional any more than we can separate our work from our personal lives. The quality of one is inextricably linked to the other: what we learn off the job translates into lessons on the job, and vice versa. The positive discipline and positive reinforcement you use with your child, for example, can be duplicated with your employees; relating better with your workers will bring positive rewards at home, as well.

Emotions need not be a problem in the workplace; the right ones augment productivity and workplace harmony, but it takes EQ to know how to manage them. Many people have the title of "manager" but are simply ineffective in their positions. Real leaders are those who actively inspire and motivate others, create teamwork, and achieve outstanding results; they model the behavior they want to see in their employees. Emotional Intelligence can move you from management to leadership, and make the people at the top sit up and take notice of your contributions to the company.

CHAPTER 2

The Science behind Emotional Intelligence

The Case for an Emotional Brain

Emotions are not just a matter of the heart. Recent advances in research have shown that they are also a result of brain biochemistry. These conclusions come from neuroscience, evolution, medicine, psychology, and management. Emotional signals in the brain are felt throughout the body — in the gut, in the heart, in the head, in the neck, and so on. These sensations are important signals: If we learn to read them, they will help us make decisions and initiate action.

Most scientists believe that the control center of emotions in the brain is the limbic system, consisting of the amygdala, the hippocampus, and other structures in the mid-brain. The limbic system stores every experience we have from the first moments of life: impressions are stored in these areas long before we acquire the verbal or higher thinking abilities to put them into words. It is this vast warehouse of feelings and impressions that provides a context or meaning for those memories.

Messages are transmitted to the brain by neurons, traveling through an electrical transmission system. In the 1970s, however, scientists discovered that our bodies also contain a chemical system for transmitting messages. This system is based on chemicals called *peptides*, which have receptors in every cell of our bodies. These highly sensitive information substances are thought to be the chemical substrates of emotion, triggering impression memories throughout our lives. Our brains are linked to all our body systems, and it is these peptides that are responsible for the emotions we "feel" in various parts of our bodies.

This chemical transmission system just described is far, far older in evolutionary history than the electrical brain. In fact, many of the same information substances found in humans are found in one-celled animals. Their presence in the most basic as well as the most complex forms of life is a clear indication of their importance.

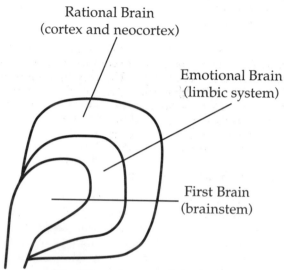

Rational Brain
(cortex and neocortex)

Emotional Brain
(limbic system)

First Brain
(brainstem)

The Three Layers of the Brain

Evolution of the Brain: Three Functional Layers

Very, very early in evolutionary history, simple "beings" had brainstems that regulated autonomic function and kept them alive. Human beings still have a *brainstem*, located just above the spinal cord, which tells our lungs to breathe and our hearts to beat. Similar in architecture to the brainstem of reptiles, the human brainstem it is sometimes called the *reflex brain* or the *first brain*. We can summon it to conscious awareness, although it usually functions automatically.

The *limbic system* or *emotional brain* is thought to have developed out of the first brain. It helps us store and remember past experiences and learn from them. The limbic system in humans is located in the approximate center of the brain; when information enters the limbic system, we experience bodily sensations, transmitted by the peptides or chemical information substances, in the form of a "reaction" to the stimulus with much more awareness of what is happening than at the level of the first brain.

Out of this limbic system came the *rational* (thinking) *brain* or thin *cortex*. The cortex enables us to comprehend sensory information and plan accordingly. The very thin outermost layer of the cortex called the *neocortex* is responsible for higher order thinking and symbolic communication, art and ideas, and long-term planning. The millions or billions of connections between the limbic brain and the thinking brain allow for the free-flow of information between these layers.

What the Three Brain Layers Do

The first brain (brain stem) is the seat of autonomic or automatic response, as well as the seat of habits. It connects us to our external world through our skin, our pores, and our nerves. It controls what impulses get recognized and passed along to the two higher levels. This brain learns through imitation, avoidance, and repetition until something becomes habitual. Information usually enters at this point without our conscious awareness. We can make much of this information conscious and use it to our benefit, as biofeedback and hypnosis have shown us.

The *emotional brain* (limbic system) helps us know what things to approach and what to avoid by guiding our preferences. As we move through life and have more experiences, we have stronger intuitions, hunches, and gut reactions because more things are stored in the limbic warehouse. We have "learned" from experience. Intuition is emotional learning gained over many years; a 14 year old has little intuition because he or she has not experienced enough life to make connections between experiences. As we mature, we accumulate more reliable emotional data that can offer us valuable clues and guide our behavior, providing we become aware of its existence and learn how to interpret it. Unfortunately, many adults have been taught to ignore this type of information.

The *rational brain* (neocortex) assists us with functions related to thinking and language: planning, questioning, making decisions, solving problems, and generating new ideas. This layer is connected to the emotional brain with millions of connections, allowing the emotional and the thinking brains to influence one another in a myriad of ways and providing rich data on which to draw conclusions and initiate action.

Our emotions have helped us immeasurably over the course of human evolution. Emotional responses are milliseconds faster than cognitive (thinking) responses; the lightning-fast reactions that bypass the rational brain centers were often survival responses for our distant ancestors. The limbic brain sends us the warning of a crisis before the rational brain can even process the incoming signal: the body has been alerted, and is ready to act on our behalf.

The emotional brain was conserved for a purpose. Today, physical survival is less of a threat than it was to primitive man, but data from the emotional brain still gives us important clues to our surroundings and the actions we need to take. Ignoring this data on purpose or because we aren't aware of it leaves us with only partial information. One of the purposes of this book is to show how emotions can be used to maximum effect without getting out of control.

Research on Emotional Intelligence

Here are some additional conclusions from evolutionary science:

- Our emotional brain and its responses have been shaped and preserved over millions of years of evolution. Humanity is "hard-wired" for emotional response!

- The facial expressions for basic emotions such as fear, sadness, disgust, anger, and pleasure are identical across cultures, indicating some inborn genetic mechanism common to the human race.

Neuroscience Research

New maps of brain circuitry tell us that the brain is affected by our emotions in two ways: First, signals travel from the first brain to the rational brain and then back to the emotional brain whenever we mull something over for a while and become increasingly angry, determined, or hurt. The "mulling over" allows us to receive more precise data and this leads to good decision-making and more effective actions.

The second pathway is the route the signal takes as it travels to the emotional brain *before* going to the rational brain. This occurs when there is an immediate and powerful recognition of a specific experience as the emotional brain makes an association with some past event; we react strongly to something without really knowing why.

The brain seems to have one memory system for ordinary facts, and another for emotionally charged events. Emotional events appear to open additional neural pathways that make them stronger in our minds, which may explain why we never forget significant events. Occasionally we are propelled into action on the basis of these few rough signals before we get confirmation from the thinking brain. We have a rational brain that keeps us from being overpowered by strong emotional reactions, but the emotional brain should not be completely overshadowed by the rational one. The key is balance.

Additional conclusions from neuroscience:

- Chemical information substances, or peptides, regulate blood flow. Blood carries glucose, the brain's fuel which is necessary for the brain to function. Blocking of emotions through trauma or denial can slow down this process, depriving the brain of nourishment and leaving it less able to think, plan, and make decisions.

- Electrical stimulation of the limbic area of the brain results in powerful emotional displays accompanied by bodily movement such as laughter or weeping; these displays of emotion are based on stored memories.

- Our brains are composed of a huge number of neural pathways and connections, making possible many subtleties of emotion and response. Emotions all have a purpose, even anger, grief, and anxiety. Denying these emotions sets up detectable molecular blockages that cause actual changes in cells: this can result in widespread physical and emotional damage over time. The peptides or chemical information substances flow more freely when we allow ourselves to express emotions such as joy or hope.

- Research in psychoneuroimmunology has shown conclusively that there is a direct link between what we think and feel and what is actually going on in our physical bodies. Our emotional and cognitive responses to events in life affect our health and our energy level — essential factors in working up to capacity.

- The term "gut reaction" can be taken literally: Our digestive tracts are particularly dense with chemical information molecules and receptors. Chemical activity is triggered by — you guessed it — strong emotions.

Medical Research

The medical laboratory also provides us with clues about how emotions operate in our brains and bodies. Consider these examples:

- Some years ago the accepted "cure" for mental illness was to do a prefrontal lobotomy (removal of a section of the brain that connects the emotional and cognitive brains). The procedure worked in that severe emotional distress was indeed relieved, but the severing of the circuitry destroyed the patient's emotional life, as well. With no ability to feel or express emotion, these patients appeared dull and lifeless.

- If the limbic brain is injured or surgically removed due to disease, the individual will lose emotional memory, and lose all feelings. He or she will have no capacity for relationships and, in fact, will not be able to remember friends and relatives. They won't be able to make even simple decisions because they no longer have any memory of likes and dislikes.

- The removal of the amygdala in animals causes them to lose fear, rage, and the urge to cooperate or to compete. This is a strong indication that the amygdala, a part of the emotional brain, controls our passions.
- Biofeedback is effective in controlling certain chronic diseases. This merging of the first brain, the limbic brain, and the thinking brain results in measurable changes at the cellular level, and improves the functions of bodily systems.

Our rational minds give us information about people and things, yet preferences and *why* we have them are based on the limbic brain's storage of emotions. Without access to that information, we are unable to make even the simplest of decisions because all choices are equal. Emotions are always present in our lives, whether we recognize them or not.

Research in Psychology

Evidence for the importance of emotions comes from the field of psychology, too. Here are some important findings:

- Stress activates a certain gene that attaches to brain DNA, causing abnormalities that lead to depression as well as other emotional difficulties. The first bad experience *feels* negative and sets up a pathway in the brain. The second experience feels worse, and after repeated experiences, the memory trace has become a superhighway for depression.
- When we are calmly energized (good stress), the brain secretes catecholamines, adrenaline, and noradrenaline. This kind of "stress" is beneficial because we can perform at our best.
- When stress is severe, the brain secretes cortisol, which intensifies sensory awareness but dulls rational thinking. When levels of this substance are high, our memory does not work well, and we make more mistakes. Cortisol levels rise when we are bored, frustrated, or highly anxious, or when we have other strong negative emotions.

- Prolonged stress in laboratory animals has been shown to actually destroy neurons, shrinking the brain's memory center.

- Experiments were performed in which people were shown shapes at a rate too quick for the shapes to register with the thinking brain. But subjects developed a preference for those shapes, even though they had no conscious awareness that they had seen them. The limbic brain perceives things more quickly, and even decides if it likes those things before the thinking brain can be engaged.

- When we look at angry or happy faces, our facial muscles change very subtly in the direction of what was viewed. These subtle changes, while not visible to our eyes, can be measured with electronic sensors.

- People showing little emotion when they first sit down to face an individual who shows a lot of emotion invariably pick up on the mood of the expressive partner. We subtly re-create in ourselves the mood of another, and may, in fact, be programmed to do so.

- Animal studies show that primates experience empathy, just as humans do. When an animal sees another of its species in distress, the primate brain has specialized neurons in the visual cortex and in the amygdala that fire only in response to particular facial expressions that convey fear, threat, or submission. This might indicate that humans also have such specialized "empathy" neurons, and that empathy is programmed into our brains.

These findings are particularly relevant in the workplace, where stress can affect the environment as well as performance. Humans are complex "wholes," programmed to respond emotionally. No one can perform their jobs apart from their emotions, but excess stress is particularly disruptive to smooth functioning, and it makes concentrated, rational thinking very difficult. "Emotionally intelligent" individuals harness these emotions and use them appropriately.

Management Science and Leadership Studies

Much evidence of Emotional Intelligence comes out of organizations: studies of leadership, management, and performance have, like laboratory research, produced much exciting new information. Here are some interesting findings.

- Studies of "think tanks," where everyone is highly intelligent, reveal that even there, some people outperform others. They are more willing to take on responsibility, are more adaptable, and more easily establish rapport with co-workers. These qualities are considered Emotional-Intelligence qualities that have little to do with IQ or technical competency.
- Research on sales managers indicates that those who are unable to handle stress oversee departments that perform poorly, while those managers who perform better under stress have high sales volume.
- CEOs judged most successful by their peers in some studies were not those rated highest in technical competency but were instead those who scored the highest in a different area: the ability to establish relationships with and inspire others.
- Men and women seem, generally, not to differ in their overall level of Emotional Intelligence. However, research often finds women to be better at empathy and social skills and men stronger in self-confidence and self-control. [These facets of EQ are the subjects of upcoming chapters.]
- Education, gender, hours worked, and geographic area did not predict sales success for those in sales. However, Emotional-Intelligence qualities of empathy, optimism, assertiveness, and self-awareness were highly predictive of sales success. Optimistic salespeople, in fact, sold 37% more insurance and were twice as likely to stick with the job as those who had pessimistic outlooks on life and work.

We make better decisions when we act on information from our feelings, our instincts, and our intuition, as well as on information coming from our rational intellect. It is our emotional brains, after all, that allow us to access memory and assign weight or preference to the choices we face at work and in our personal lives. It is our Emotional Intelligence that guides us in controlling or accessing emotions when we must adapt to change, get along with others, or deal with stress. Performance and leadership in any organizational setting are both influenced by EQ.

CHAPTER 3

Assessing Emotional Intelligence

The purpose of this Pocket Guide is to help you improve your leadership skills by focusing on emotional competencies that affect success in the workplace and in the world at large. Before you can identify what you need to improve, however, you must know where you are now. This chapter will help you assess your Emotional Intelligence and then target areas where it can be strengthened. It concludes with several practical suggestions.

The checklists that follow have been used quite successfully with leaders who are engaged in the developmental processes of coaching and training in order to improve leadership. They are valuable personal tools for managers seeking to gain an understanding of their strengths and weaknesses in the area of Emotional Intelligence, in order to chart a course for personal improvement and business success.

1. Rating EQ: Self-Assessment

The Self-Assessment Checklist is based on the six-facet model of Emotional Intelligence introduced in Chapter 1. It will point out to you those facets of Emotional Intelligence in which you have opportunity for improvement. Chapters 5–10 include "Suggestion. . ." sections with activities designed to strengthen specific areas.

EQ SELF-ASSESSMENT CHECKLIST

Rate each question below on a scale of 1–5, according to how true it is of you.

1	2	3	4	5
virtually never				virtually always

_____ 1) I am aware of the physical reactions (twinges, aches, sudden changes) that signal a "gut reaction."

_____ 2) I readily admit mistakes and apologize.

_____ 3) I let go of problems, anger, or hurts from the past and I can move beyond these.

_____ 4) I generally have an accurate idea of how another person perceives me during a particular interaction.

_____ 5) I have several important things in my life that I am enthusiastic about, and I let it show.

_____ 6) I can easily meet and initiate conversation with new people when I have to.

_____ 7) I take a break or use another active method of increasing energy when I sense that my energy level is getting low.

_____ 8) I have little trouble taking prudent risks.

_____ 9) I "open up" with people appropriately — not too much but enough so that I don't come across as cold and distant.

_____ 10) I can engage in an interaction with another and pretty well size-up that person's mood based on non-verbal signals.

_____ 11) Others usually feel inspired and encouraged after talking to me.

EQ SELF-ASSESSMENT CHECKLIST (continued)

___ 12) I have no trouble making presentations in front of groups or conducting meetings.

___ 13) I take time every day for quiet reflection.

___ 14) I take initiative and move ahead on tasks that need to be done.

___ 15) I refrain from making up my mind on issues and expressing my opinion until I have all the facts.

___ 16) I have a number of people I can turn to, and I ask for their help when I need it.

___ 17) I try to find the positive in any given situation.

___ 18) I can deal calmly, sensitively, and proactively with the emotional displays of others.

___ 19) I can usually identify the emotion I am feeling at any given moment.

___ 20) I am generally comfortable in new situations.

___ 21) I neither bury my anger nor let it explode on others.

___ 22) I can show empathy and match my feelings with those of another person in an interaction.

___ 23) I can keep going on a big project, despite obstacles.

___ 24) I am respected and liked by others, even when they don't agree with me.

___ 25) I am clear about my own goals and values.

___ 26) I express my views honestly and thoughtfully, without being pushy.

___ 27) I am good at managing my moods, and I seldom bring negative emotions to work.

___ 28) I focus my full attention on another person when I listen to them.

___ 29) I believe the work I do day-to-day has meaning and value to society.

___ 30) I can effectively persuade others to adopt my point of view without coercing them.

Scoring the Self-Assessment Checklist

1. Enter your ratings for each numbered question in the category where it appears.

2. Add the ratings for each category to obtain a total for that specific facet of EQ.

Self-Awareness:
  1 _____
  7 _____
  13 _____
  19 _____
  25 _____
Total Self-Awareness _____

Empathy:
  4 _____
  10 _____
  16 _____
  22 _____
  28 _____
Total Empathy _____

Self-Confidence:
  2 _____
  8 _____
  14 _____
  20 _____
  26 _____
Total Self-Confidence _____

Motivation:
  5 _____
  11 _____
  17 _____
  23 _____
  29 _____
Total Motivation _____

Self-Control:
  3 _____
  9 _____
  15 _____
  21 _____
  27 _____
Total Self-Control _____

Social Competency:
  6 _____
  12 _____
  18 _____
  24 _____
  30 _____
Total Social Competency _____

Interpreting the Score

Your score on each of the six facets will fall somewhere between 5 and 25 points. Circle any facet where your score was below 20: This indicates an area that you can improve. Read the rest of this book and resolve especially to practice the ideas listed in the chapter devoted to it. Your overall Emotional Intelligence will improve as you work on that particular area.

Other opportunities for improvement can be found in any individual question from the Checklist on which you scored a 4 or below. Circle those questions; a rating of "3" is average, but if you have Emotional Intelligence, you are above average. So you need to target that area for improvement and turn it into a specific goal.

Effective leaders are generally high in all six areas. If you want your career and your relationships to soar, think of this Pocket Guide as a workbook, and make a commitment to do something to improve your weaknesses each day. Ideas for improvement in personal/self areas can be found in Chapters 5–7.

Obtaining Feedback from Others

Other people have much to teach us about ourselves. Examining our own behavior is crucial, but while most of us know our own strengths and weaknesses reasonably well, there are countless little things of which we are often unaware. The way other people perceive us has a great deal to do with how effective we are in any interaction, and we can't know for sure how we are coming across unless we ask for feedback. Hearing the observations of others with whom we interact will increase our self-awareness. The checklist below will assist in obtaining feedback

2.   Rating EQ: Leadership Assessment

The Leadership Assessment Checklist is also a good source of information for personal growth. It is often helpful to compare the way we rate ourselves and the way others rate us on the very same items, but other people can only indirectly assess our "Self" competencies. They can, however, judge us fairly accurately in terms of social and leadership skills. The questions on the list that follows are different from the Self-Assessment Checklist: The Leadership Assessment Checklist pertains to such EQ competencies as empathy, motivation, optimism, and social competency, as well as leadership and team-building skills such as employee empowerment, feedback, and conflict-resolution, described in Chapters 8–10 and especially in Chapters 11 and 12. Give copies of the Checklist to peers and associates, employees, friends, supervisors, your mentor, and to anyone else who can provide a snapshot of your behavior to help increase your self-awareness. Make sure they have a place to return this easily and anonymously, and give them a deadline date.

LEADERSHIP ASSESSMENT CHECKLIST

Please rate _____ (insert your name) on each of the following statements by using the rating scale below.

1	2	3	4	5
virtually never				virtually always

_____ 1) Stands behind employees, backing their decisions and advocating for them to higher management.

_____ 2) Knows how to delegate tasks but remain available for consultation.

_____ 3) Takes disciplinary action promptly and fairly, without being overly harsh or demeaning.

_____ 4) Sets high performance standards for self and subordinates.

_____ 5) As soon as he/she is aware of a problem, sits down with a subordinate who has not met expectations, coaches them, and works with them to perform better.

_____ 6) Provides frequent feedback to employees on how they are doing their job.

LEADERSHIP ASSESSMENT CHECKLIST (continued)

_____ 7) Uses more praise and positive feedback than negative feedback.

_____ 8) Refrains from letting some employees get away with less effort than others.

_____ 9) Can persuade others to adopt his/her point of view without coercion.

_____ 10) Makes positive use of conflict by encouraging discussion of differing points of view.

_____ 11) Keeps employees informed at all times about things that might affect them.

_____ 12) Takes the long-term view, without getting too focused on strictly short-term results.

_____ 13) Listens well and shows empathy and concern when I have a problem.

_____ 14) Has an open-door policy and makes himself/herself available to the staff when needed.

_____ 15) Refuses to tolerate bigotry or narrow-mindedness among the staff.

_____ 16) Helps employees discover their own solutions, without automatically providing answers

_____ 17) Keeps conflict among employees from festering or getting out of control, and instead works to reach a common understanding.

_____ 18) Tries to be patient with staff when implementing a change, knowing that there is an adjustment period.

_____ 19) Actively looks for ways to challenge and develop all workers.

_____ 20) "Opens up" to others appropriately — not too much, but enough to assure them that he/she is not cold and distant.

Using Your Leadership Assessment Checklist Results

Calculate an average score on each question by averaging all responses on each of the twenty questions. For example, if you received five completed checklists, calculate an average for the five on Question 1, Question 2, etc. Pay particular attention to any question with a rating of less than 4.0. The further it is under 4, the greater the need for work in that area. Make this a personal developmental goal for your own career.

In addition, examine individual questions from individual raters where you scored lower than 4. Perhaps some people believe that you do need work in that area. Again, this is helpful information and guides you as you develop personal goals.

Setting Personal Goals

Based on the assessment you performed on yourself and the feedback you obtained from others, what three goals would you most like to concentrate on for your personal and professional leadership development as they pertain to Emotional Intelligence? Write those below and refer to them often to guide your efforts as you study the upcoming pages.

_____

_____

_____

_____

_____

_____

_____

CHAPTER 4

The Fundamentals of Emotional Intelligence

There are several highly effective ways of improving your Emotional Intelligence. These are called "Fundamentals" because they are helpful in developing multiple facets of EQ. When used consistently, they can also help you improve in both the Self and Social dimensions. Remember these and refer back to them often throughout the remainder of the book.

Self Fundamentals: Understanding and Accepting Ourselves

Keep a Journal.

For 10 minutes each morning or each evening, *write* whatever you want. Do not get out your laptop, and don't sit at your desktop computer! The pen and the paper are essential, and though it is a slower process, you'll get more benefit from doing it this way because you will be more intimately connected with your words. Journal writing can be totally open-ended with no specific plan, or built around a theme. The meaning in your writing will not be evident until you have entered your thoughts faithfully for two or more weeks and you can look back over all you have written. The content does not have to be profound, but the physical act of writing is linked to memory — particularly emotional memory, and your heart. Do not try to organize your writing; let the words flow. Resolve to continue this for at least six months.

Use a Programmed Relaxation Response.

Practice at least 10 minutes a day for two weeks, every day. Choose a very calming image (a lake, a mountain, etc.), a calming sound (the tide or a ticking clock), a word or short phrase (*peace; I am calm*). Hold the image in your mind for the full 10 minutes. Your mind will probably stray, but don't chastise yourself if it does. Remain calm, and simply refocus on your calming image or message and let other thoughts fade away. This will help you practice turning on calming physical reactions to stressful situations.

After two weeks of faithful practice, try beginning your session by imagining a difficult situation. As you feel yourself getting angry or anxious, shift your mind back to your programmed relaxation response. Practice this variation 10 minutes a day for two more weeks. Then try your programmed response in real situations in which you feel yourself getting anxious or angry.

Write yourself a "Positive" Script.

This is a positive internal monologue you program for yourself. Our minds are never still. The trouble is, we often let negative messages drift through our minds and take over — negative images that reduce our energy and bring about the things we most fear: failure and rejection. Keep your script short. Here is an example:

> *I have a lot of talent and enthusiasm. People find me likable, and I am very good at making sales. I work hard to please my customers, and they are loyal to me. I want to be the best sales rep in this region. I know I can do it! Increased sales will bring me greater financial rewards, make me proud, and get me noticed. I believe in myself, my team, and this company, and I know I can make a difference — today and every day.*

Keep a copy in your desk drawer and read it over every morning and at lunch. Repeat the words mentally or read the Positive Script during stressful times. Do this religiously for a few weeks, and you will probably only find you need to repeat it when things seem particularly tough or stressful.

Pre-Plan how you will respond to Stressful Situations.

We can be more prepared to deal with emotions if we plan ahead of time how we will respond, especially when we are angry or depressed. Like having a mapped escape route in case of fire, you increase the likelihood that you will survive the negative emotion if you plan ahead. Identify a place where you can retreat: a "safe place" that you can go: one on the job and one at home. Can you get outdoors for a short time? Is there a safe or calming room where you can find solitude and solace? What will you do there? Plan a calming activity to deal with anger, and an energizing or funny activity to combat sadness.

Look at the situation from a different perspective: Reframe.

We often get in trouble because we make assumptions about someone else's emotions or intentions. Many times we think "the worst." However, we should challenge the thoughts that stimulate our negative thinking. Is there another explanation for the same set of circumstances? Instead of letting anger, hurt, or worry take over, we ought to redefine, or take a different view: *I'm better off* or *Maybe she had a good reason* or *He probably didn't mean it like that.*

You might need a partner to help you look at the situation a little differently. For example: Sadness over the loss of a job can be reframed by thinking of all the ways the job really did not suit you; the job was okay, but it was not perfect. And ask yourself, *What did I learn from this job and from this experience of losing it?* You can choose to dwell on the loss and stay depressed, or you can reframe and remember the positive things you derived from the experience.

Make a Mental Video of the situation as you would like it to unfold.

If we can imagine it, we can create it. That's what research tells us. We must first be able to clearly see the end we want to achieve. Close your eyes and *really see* yourself going through all the steps leading to that desired end, as if you were viewing a video of someone else. View it in as much detail as possible: Where are you? Who is there? What are each of you doing and saying? Replay your mental video over and over, and sharpen the images each time. More than a static visualization, this method of learning actually programs your neural circuitry step-by-step, so that when you begin the action steps, you have already created the "highway" for the neurons to travel. Star athletes regularly use this method to achieve great results, and you can do the same thing. In fact, the more clearly you can see your video, the more motivation it will offer you.

Social Fundamentals: The Fundamental of Social Interaction

When you have a high degree of understanding and acceptance of yourself, you are ready to move on to Emotional Intelligence in the Social dimension. These next fundamentals have to do with social interactions. If practiced faithfully, the techniques can elevate the level of success in the Social dimension and help you raise the Emotional Intelligence of those you lead.

- **Walk in Their Shoes.** This exercise will help create empathy and understanding. Make yourself write a paragraph about anyone you are having difficulty with (a peer, a subordinate, or a superior). Write what you know about the person — their interests, their background, their difficulties, etc., and try to concentrate on why they may be acting the way they are. Write in the first person, pretending you are them. As you interact with this person, continue to try to find out more about them, and continue writing about them. You will find that you approach them with more understanding and empathy. As you interact with them more positively, their behavior toward you will likewise improve, and the interactions will become smoother.

- **"Process" Comments.** Most of us focus our remarks strictly on content when we are interacting with others. Process comments, however, focus on the *reasons underlying certain behaviors* that we observe; these are comments that focus on the "why" or "how" of behavior, not the "what." When we comment on or point out the *process*, we help team members grow and deal directly with any possible conflict. A process comment focuses attention on some inconsistency ("The team is saying one thing, but it is doing another"); the method by which members work to solve a problem ("Some people do not seem fully engaged in this task"); or some underlying reason for behavior ("I wonder if this reluctance is because some of us are still upset about the new leave policy?"). When others do not seem to see that anything is wrong, a process comment can help bring out those things no one wants to mention. Good process comments usually begin with the leader's observation, stated as a description rather than an evaluation. A comment such as, "What's happening here?" or "Let's talk more about how we have been working together on this," can open dialogue. When a team begins to discover the ways it has been unproductive, members can resolve to change behavior and become more effective.

- **The "Three-Step" Method.** The Three-Step method is an excellent way to deal with conflict or potential conflict. It works whether you are a participant in the conflict or a third-party peacemaker. The steps are simple:
  1. Offer to hear the other person's side of the story *first*. (For third party mediation: Ask one party to go first while the other listens carefully.) Really listen, without interrupting or getting defensive. Agree with anything you can about what they have said.
  2. Tell them your side of the story without laying blame. (For third-party mediation: Ask the other party to tell their story. Each person must listen carefully to the other, in turn). The other party is likely to listen more closely if you allow them to go first and model good listening.
  3. Use a problem-solving approach: "How can we work this out so this doesn't happen again?" or "What can we do now to salvage this project?"

- **Look for Similar/Look for Good.** To make interactions run smoother, we need to look for the characteristics in others that are *the same* as ours and that are *good*. These connections are often found at the emotional level. Much of our culture is strongly shaped by the mass media, which focuses our attention on what's "wrong," what's abnormal, and what's different.

To improve Emotional Intelligence, we must look for common ground. After every interaction, force yourself to focus on the interaction just completed. What common ground did you see? Make it a game to always be able to find something, even something small, that you and the other person both share. Make it a habit to find the good that others are doing and comment frequently on those behaviors, being liberal with thanks and praise. Remember the importance of empathy and the need to be aware of what the other person is feeling so you can respond appropriately.

CHAPTER 5

The Role of Self-Awareness in Emotional Intelligence

You are sitting at your desk reviewing the latest sales figures, and they look pretty good. Although you are probably not aware of any strong feelings, you know you are feeling satisfied and calm. Your phone rings. You pick it up and hear the angry voice of a client, one of your biggest accounts, who is threatening to go with another supplier because a shipment you said you were sending did not arrive. Immediately, you become aware that you are no longer calm — your heart is pounding, you feel yourself starting to sweat, and your breathing is quicker — you know you are feeling anxious.

Self-awareness is a simple phrase for a complicated set of information. It refers to an awareness of ourselves on many different levels: our body and our physical reactions; our emotions, preferences, and intentions; our goals and values; and our knowledge about how we come across to others. The more self-awareness we have, the more easily we can adjust our responses to others, and the more mutually satisfying our interactions and transactions. Tuning in to ourselves and becoming more aware of what we are experiencing as we are experiencing it improves Emotional Intelligence.

All emotions are composed of bodily energy at the cellular level. Emotions are a form of data, and even emotions that do not give us "pleasure" provide us with important information. All emotions are therefore positive for the information they provide; as we learn to tune in to the messages they send us, we become healthier.

Feel What You Are Feeling

Being aware of an emotion is not the same as expressing it. We can make a conscious choice about how to respond or whether to respond at all, but we can only make these choices if we are aware of the emotions we are experiencing. Awareness opens up new possibilities for behavior.

If we are not aware of what is happening within us, our responses might only be automatic — not guided by reason or by intuition. If, for example, we begin our day with a negative experience, it can leave us irritable and unpleasant, affecting our dealings with other people, and we might not even be aware of it. When someone finally calls our attention to the "blow up" or irritability, we are surprised into awareness. Once we figure out what we are experiencing, we feed this data to the thinking brain and make a more conscious effort to change the negative outlook into a positive one.

Not being aware of our "self" can also get us into trouble when someone "pushes our buttons." We blow up out of proportion to the situation because a limbic memory was triggered. Sometimes we revert back to responses learned in childhood — shrinking when a supervisor yells at us, perhaps, because of an old memory of verbal abuse. Being self-aware is the key to self-control and freedom of action; out of it can come empathy and genuine human connection.

We are often not aware of what we are feeling until the feelings become quite strong. The truth, however, is that we are always "feeling" something just as we are always thinking something. If we want to grow in intelligence, we must pay more attention to the cognitive process, and if we want to become more emotionally intelligent, we need to pay attention and let ourselves truly *feel*. Tuning in to our physical self is where self-awareness must begin.

Serious emotional or physical trauma can cause an individual to "turn off" their awareness of what is happening to them — a way of coping that can become an emotional "handicap" carried into adulthood that stifles ability and leadership potential. The damage can be corrected with positive

elationships in adulthood, a desire to change, and therapy.
Adult brains have the capacity to relearn emotional patterns
through persistence and patience.

The Language of Feelings

What words do you use to describe *your* emotions? Many
people are unable to give labels to their feelings beyond a few
basic ones, such as *anger, worry, sadness,* or *happiness.* (The
"negative" emotions are the ones we seem to remember, no
matter what!) Since self-awareness is an important part of
Emotional Intelligence and being in touch with what we are
feeling is critical to being self-aware, we need a language or a
framework to comfortably describe our emotions.

Emotional energy can expand, giving us a push, or it can
contract, pulling us back. The following model represents
direction and intensity of energy for the most common
emotions. Because there are many millions of neural pathways,
many combinations, subtleties, and synonyms of the basic
emotions listed on the model are possible.

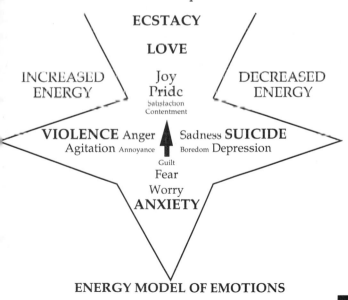

ENERGY MODEL OF EMOTIONS

In the preceding model, the left-hand point represents increased energy which can overflow the body and become other-directed; violence against persons or property is the extreme form of this. The closed point, however, signifies this is a closed pathway that leads to a diminishing of the self. The right-hand point represents the other extreme — reduced energy flow. Again, this is a closed pathway, which closes off the self and in the extreme can lead to suicide. The emotional states of anxiety at the bottom of the model represent a push-pull toward action, or both an increase and decrease in energy — emotions that can distract us and keep us in a state of uncertainty. The further an individual moves from the center toward the left, the right, or the bottom point on the model the more he or she experiences a more extreme form of that family of emotions.

Only those emotions at the top, open end of the model are both expansive for the self and are experienced as positive. They can be self-directed or other-directed emotions. The left, right, and bottom directions are all necessary and normal, but we generally perceive the three points of the model as negative. Without awareness and appropriate handling of the emotion we are experiencing, our limbic brains can easily propel us far down one of the points. An extreme in any of these can be dangerous to ourselves or others. The points are dead-ends and are rarely fully reached by emotionally intelligent people with self-awareness. Our thinking brains can help point us back towards the center of the model and transform the energy back to the upward direction. But we need to spend some time periodically moving near the points to increase our awareness of what's happening around us, gather strength, and make the changes necessary to get ourselves back on track.

The Energy Model, as it is shown, is a flat diagram with two dimensions on the page. However, the actions of emotion can really be considered as being three-dimensional. If you can envision the left and right points as bending around backward so they touch in back, this demonstrates how close the strong emotions of rage and depression can be — how people cross over from violence and agitation to suicide. Extreme cases like murder-suicide demonstrate this relationship and are a vivid example of emotionally unintelligent behavior.

How Emotions Manifest Themselves

If we do not pay attention to feelings and learn how to label and deal with them through better communication, they reveal themselves in the body: fatigue, lack of concentration, pain, and poor health. If we focus on emotions and allow ourselves to feel them, little by little, they will deepen in intensity and help us learn and connect with others. Suppressing emotions, both the positive and negative ones, seems to deny our brains access to important natural chemicals. The alternative, prescription and illicit drugs, are poor substitutes for the natural chemicals that are released through emotional experience and expression.

Suggestions for Increasing Self-Awareness

Look inward. We are bombarded with messages about the outside world, yet we often fail to communicate with the world inside ourselves. Here are some ways to get to know who *we* are:

1. *Journal.* (EQ Fundamentals, Chapter 4) Also try writing about a specific question: "What's important to me?" After you spend a number of days writing on this topic, begin to ask yourself: "Is how I spend my time reflective of what's important to me?"

2. Get in touch with your own work preferences as a clue to your passions. Instead of just taking on any project, work to become part of those activities you love. If you have lost touch with yourself to the extent that you don't remember what you love anymore, write about what you really loved in the past.

3. Become aware of *where* in the body you are feeling an emotion: the neck, shoulders, jaw, throat, abdomen, chest. If you tune in to your physical responses, you can guide the energy and respond flexibly, rather than be in the grip of the emotion. To get the most out of our energy, we want its intensity — but we should not let it control us. (More about this in Chapter 6.)

Suggestions for Increasing Self-Awareness

4. Develop a habit of self-observation and self-curiosity: Visualize yourself as if you are observing a third person. Think about your own thinking. Rather than allowing yourself to operate on autopilot, tune in to yourself and your emotional stream of consciousness, and thus identify your subtle moods.

5. *Make* yourself spend 15–20 minutes daily on self-reflection and awareness-building. Schedule this in your planner and don't let other things interfere with it. Do something silent, pleasant, and relaxing, such as a quiet walk, and let your thoughts wander at will.

6. During your commute to work, think ahead about two situations that you will encounter during the day: one that will produce no strong emotion, and another that will result in some emotion. As you live the experience of each situation, pay attention to yourself: How are you reacting? What's going on in your body and in your head? For at least two weeks, keep a small log at your desk and write down information about each of these areas as they relate to a specific situation:

Situation	Heart rate	Breathing	Perspir-ation	Muscle tightness	Feelings

7. When you sense tension or low energy, fix it immediately. Take a few bites of a healthy snack (junk food does not count!), get some fresh air, take a little walk for a change of scenery, stand up and stretch and shrug your shoulders a few times, or do a few twists. We need a creative pause of two to three minutes every 20–30 minutes to keep energy high.

Suggestions for Increasing Self-Awareness

8. Increasing self-awareness means that you will also become more aware of "the bad stuff," things you don't particularly like about yourself. Challenges and problems are normal, so accept the fact that you will never get to be wise enough and powerful enough to eliminate flaws. Being self-aware means that when you have a problem, you can turn it into a challenge — an opportunity to grow. Here are some ideas:

   • Define your problem very carefully. Ask yourself *What's really going on here?*

   • Brainstorm new solutions, including silly ones (they often have useful elements).

   • Weigh the pros and cons of your ideas. Try to balance your brain and your heart. What is your heart or your "gut" telling you? Is your alternative truly something you can commit to with your whole being? Facts and figures are not the only things that matter.

   • Live with your preferred solution for a while, rather than jump in to take immediate action. Let your intuition take over, and incubate your plan for a few days. If you still feel committed with your heart as well as your head, *then...*

   • Take action. Evaluate how it's going as you implement your plan, and modify only as needed.

Ask for Feedback. Interestingly, self-awareness comes not only from careful observation of ourselves but from those around us. In fact, significant others in our lives can provide valuable data to increase our self-awareness. Many organizations make use of this idea through some form of 360-degree feedback in which customers, peers, and subordinates, as well as supervisors, provide feedback on how you are doing.

If your organization does not use such a system of performanc review (or if it is done badly), you can still obtain valuable information by soliciting feedback from people you know through the Leadership Assessment Checklist included in Chapter 3. Such feedback will increase your awareness by reducing blind spots.

Additional Suggestions for Increasing Self-Awareness

Look for Feedback. Trusted friends and colleagues can help us see how we come across to other people.

1. Make arrangements to talk with someone who listens well and who can be completely honest with you — someone whom you can talk to regularly about yourself. Get them to help you look at yourself objectively in several broad areas. Discuss whether or not you are focused on your purpose, and evaluate whether or not what you are doing is helping you fulfill the purpose as you have defined it. Having such an advisor will help improve your health and your career.

2. Ask your advisor to point out any destructive patterns he or she sees in you. For example, do you frequently use avoidance, sarcasm, cynicism, or demands when you meet challenges? If so, such behaviors will get in the way of your purpose, and awareness of these patterns is the first step toward controlling them. Start noticing, and keep a log of when the problem behavior occurs.

Additional Suggestions for Increasing Self-Awareness

3. You can also enhance self-awareness by teaming up with a trusted colleague on the job. Make a point of having lunch with that person on a regular basis in order to exchange helpful information and observations on each other's behavior. Take turns being in the hot seat.

4. Ask about another person's perception of you, and don't be afraid or threatened by what they might say. Look at it as an opportunity to increase your self-knowledge and awareness. If you are too nervous about what they might say and lack the confidence to ask, the next chapter on self-confidence can help you.

CHAPTER 6

The Role of Self-Confidence in Emotional Intelligence

Karen performed well as assistant operations manager at a manufacturing facility. She was skilled at her job and did what she was told, but her manager noticed that she seldom took initiative. She seemed hesitant to move ahead with new things and often needed extra encouragement. Karen was capable, but did not seem to have confidence in her abilities. Her manager believed that this lack of confidence was holding her back from taking on additional responsibility and moving ahead in her career.

Self-confidence is one of the six important facets of Emotional Intelligence. It is almost always present in people we admire and respect who "have their act together." We admire individuals who display a positive attitude toward themselves without being arrogant.

Self-confidence is a positive and balanced attitude having to do with the Self dimension. It consists of a basic belief that we can do what is needed to produce the desired outcome. When obstacles occur, a person with a confident attitude continues to work to overcome the barriers, whereas someone lacking in self-confidence is not likely to persevere and might not even begin something. Overcoming barriers and giving ourselves credit for what we have achieved — no matter how insignificant to others — are important ways to build self-confidence. Experiencing small successes will build larger ones.

Confidence or Arrogance?

Low self-confidence affects job performance, but another kind of self-confidence problem is equally incompatible with EQ: arrogance. Over-confidence or pseudo-confidence is destructive, and does not belong in today's organization. In fact, people who are domineering and who think they are entitled to make decisions without regard to how they will affect others are as ineffective as their low-confidence peers, because arrogance creates resentment. Employees and peers who resent this lack of consideration and respect will hold bac on productivity: Where's the incentive? the appreciation? The will make minimal efforts, but don't count on them pitching in in a crisis!

People who lack true self-confidence leave clues: difficulty admitting mistakes, an unwillingness to apologize, pushiness, and bragging are all signs of a confidence problem. While bragging might look a lot like confidence on the surface, peopl who are truly self-confident have no need to brag; those who do are often trying to convince themselves of their own worth. And when we are so worried about looking incompetent in the eyes of others that we can't admit our own shortcomings, we are not likely to take advantage of coaching and advice from peers and potential mentors. But if we are to develop high EQ and become successful, this is exactly what we must do!

Low Self-Confidence

We judge self-confidence by whether or not someone is able to meet our gaze, by whether they speak up, by the way they walk and carry their bodies, and by how much initiative and determination they display. Anxiety or worry are the emotions most associated with a lack of self-confidence, but low self-confidence is also associated with depression. It is hard to hide a lack of confidence: the signs are obvious.

Some would argue that self-confidence does not matter so much when you are the manager. After all, even a manager low in self-confidence can still give orders, monitor people and projects, and meet deadlines, right? Actually, adopting domineering behaviors is one way people deal with low self-confidence. These tactics, however, simply *don't work with today's workforce*. People do not respect managers who are timi and passive, but the management skills that are needed today also have little to do with command and control abilities. We put our faith only in leaders who believe in themselves: they inspire and motivate us.

How often are we, as managers, called upon to:

- make a formal or informal presentation to our superiors?
- advocate for a particular need or for an employee?
- be persuasive in advancing an argument or leading a change?
- inspire (not command!) our people to work harder?
- make a firm decision and move ahead with implementation?
- overcome an obstacle?
- take a risk?

All the things listed above and many other activities we do every day depend on having a high level of self-confidence to do them well. If we are low in this aspect of Emotional Intelligence, we must set a goal for ourselves to build it up by doing some of the things listed below.

Suggestions for Overcoming Low Self-Esteem

You can increase your self-esteem! Here are a few good suggestions:

1. Write yourself a *Positive Script* — an internal monologue that bolsters your ego. (Refer to the Fundamentals section in Chapter 4 for details on how to do this.)

2. Carefully think about and devise a mission statement for yourself. Keep a copy in your desk drawer and take it out several times during the day to read. It will help remind you of what you are about, and give you a sense of quiet pride. Here is an example of such a statement, which can inspire you to write your own.

I believe in myself and I believe that I have a purpose on this earth. My values include spending time with my family, doing my very best to give my employer a hard day's work, and giving back to my community. I love the challenge of investigating and solving thorny problems in medical billing, and being a source of information and inspiration for less experienced employees. Dealing with human relations problems is sometimes a challenge for me, but I will continue to try to listen with concern and compassion before judging. I value participation among my employees and strive not to give all the answers or make all the decisions. I will not allow my work to take up all of my time and I will spend quality time each day with my family. Each and every week I will do something to give back to the community and try to make the world a better place.

Write your own inspiring mission statement below. If your mission in life does not coincide with where you are right now in your job or personal life, plan to spend some time contemplating what you really want by becoming more self-aware [see previous chapter]. Maybe it's also time to get some professional career or personal counseling to help you clarify what you want. When our circumstances differ substantially from our true calling, it is hard to develop self-confidence or to be high in any other dimension of Emotional Intelligence.

Suggestions for Overcoming Low Self-Esteem

MY PERSONAL MISSION STATEMENT:

_____

_____

_____

_____

_____

_____

3. In the blanks below, list five things you do very well
    (anything from gardening to making PowerPoint
    presentations) and two things you do less well. Spend
    time considering how you can do more of the things you
    do well and less of the things you do badly. Eliminate
    things from your life that make you feel incompetent, _or_
    make a commitment to getting instruction to become
    competent in these areas.

    What are YOUR top-five things you do well? (This might
    even provide a clue to your true mission.)

    1. _____

    2. _____

    3. _____

    4. _____

    5. _____

    What two things are you currently doing that you do
    poorly, and how can you reduce or eliminate those?

    1. _____

    2. _____

Suggestions for Overcoming Low Self-Esteem

4. Develop a *Mind Video* that shows you progressing toward your goal. (Refer to the Fundamentals Section in Chapter 4 for details.)

5. Work on your image. We feel better and more self-confident when we know we look good. Everyone can make the most of what they have, without being a model of physical attractiveness. It costs you nothing to smile, be neat, meet people's eyes, and carry yourself proudly.

6. *Pretend* that you have lots of self-confidence. "Fake it 'til you make it" really does work. You can do it in this way: Develop a clear mental video image of yourself acting in a highly confident way in personal or job situations, much the way your ideal leader might act in those situations. Resolve to act exactly like this for three full days, *as if you were the character in a play*. Act calmly self-assured. Continue to replay your mind video between acts of your play. Research shows that most people actually feel more confident after pretending they were confident.

7. Identify someone you have been too timid around. Write a script for how you might speak up around that person. Practice your script aloud, in private. Get your thoughts out with some conviction, and don't worry about the words. Seek out this person and state the opinions or feelings you previously did not voice. Never state your opinion in a dogmatic or aggressive way, but merely a business-like way. For example:

   "Karen, I've been thinking about the plans we discussed last week, and wanted to share my opinion. I think we should try to do this project in-house, rather than go with a subcontractor, and here's why..."

Suggestions for Overcoming Low Self-Esteem

8. If you don't speak up in meetings, you must begin doing so. Resolve to contribute something in every meeting you attend, beyond merely asking a question. Try this: Get an agenda ahead of time. Pick an issue you know about or care about, and plan ahead what you can say in that meeting. If you don't know much about the issues, do your homework to learn more by researching or talking to colleagues. Rehearse what you will say. Plant the thought in your mind: "I can do it, I will do it." Speak up early in the meeting before you have a chance to talk yourself out of it. Voicing your opinion and being involved leads to greater self-confidence and greater leadership ability.

9. Seek out opportunities to make presentations. Take anything that you do well or know quite a bit about and offer to present that subject at a staff meeting or another appropriate small-group forum. If you start out with a small audience, it becomes progressively easier to present to larger or more challenging groups, such as your Board of Directors. Prepare carefully ahead of time, and rehearse what you will say. Smile and take a deep breath before you start, because we often run out of oxygen when we are nervous.

10. It's okay to break certain rules if you have to to achieve some greater good. Use good judgment here about which ones you break, and always have a good reason and documentation if anyone calls you on it later. A great deal of confidence and power comes from exercising independent judgment, rather than following arbitrary rules to the letter.

Suggestions for Overcoming Low Self-Esteem

11. Break down any larger goal into steps. "Increasing confidence" is far too big a goal; it's more like a vision. Break this vision into steps like this: "I'll call this person this morning" or "I'll make a comment in this afternoon's meeting" or "I'll go to this place to look for a job."

12. Keep a log of each step you take toward your bigger goal or vision. With each step write a short phrase about how this increased your confidence. Try to tie each individual action to how it felt. The more you can connect each individual experience with your goal, the closer you are toward achieving your goal.

13. Think of a current problem situation you are facing. What do you think, how do you feel, and what are you currently doing? Write this down in a few sentences. Now, write down as completely as possible, like a story, what you'd like to do, think, and feel instead. Rehearse your new story in your mind just like a video. The next time you get in this situation, you'll have a new response to try instead when you feel the old pattern coming on.

A leader cannot be more concerned with being liked than with getting the job done. Therefore, leaders have to be very secure. They must be able to say NO, set high standards, confront when necessary, take charge, and hold people accountable — not always pleasant things to do. As we make small conscious steps toward increasing self-confidence, the momentum will build and we will see even greater increases.

What about Overconfidence?

You can be assertive and business-like without being aggressive and running over others. Self-confidence is *not* the same as being pushy or arrogant, having all the answers, or easily telling people off. Such emotionally *unintelligent* behavior has to do with either covering up insecurities or being haughty — genuinely believing we are better or smarter than others.

To determine if you have this type of a confidence problem, ask yourself: "Do I frequently take a very strong stand on issues?" "Am I the first to speak up with an opinion?" " Do I often cut off further discussion in favor of my position?" "Do I spend more time talking than I do listening?" If you answer "yes" to one or more of these questions, you might be running over other people. Keep in mind that emotionally intelligent self-confidence stops short of overconfidence.

If we are overconfident, people will accuse us of being pushy. We seldom apologize or say we are wrong. We might even pride ourselves in this, but others don't like this behavior. In fact, the "confidence" of the know-it-all is a barrier to good communication and the development of positive relationships within the organization. The bottom-line is: Most people resent know-it-alls and they are unwilling to give overconfident, bossy people what they want, whereas they will work diligently for someone who has genuine give-and-take confidence.

People with a genuine belief in themselves do not have trouble admitting they are wrong and apologizing for mistakes. We all make mistakes, and plenty of them. People who stick to their guns and won't admit they are wrong are those who suffer with the burdensome and erroneous belief that saying "I was wrong and I'm sorry" diminishes them in some way. There is usually some basic insecurity they are covering up.

Be honest as you examine yourself. Coming off as overconfident might have become such a habit that you do not even realize you do this. That's why you should seek out 360° feedback and comments from others. (See the previous chapter on increasing awareness.) *What is it you are covering up or worried about that makes you need to push people around?*

We need to let go of the need to have all the answers, and learn to be a little more vulnerable. Then we can move from arrogance to confidence, and *gain* respect rather than lose it.

Genuine confidence helps us balance our needs with those of other people, and this will lead to more success in the Social dimension.

Suggestions for Overcoming Aggressive Overconfidence

If you think you are overconfident — even just a little — here are some things you can do to become more balanced:

1. Set a personal goal for the next week to voice your opinion *last* in all formal and informal meetings in which you participate. This requires you to be quieter and listen to others. Make yourself ask questions of others. When it is your turn, formulate your response in a way that is not so extreme. A less dogmatic opinion will allow more room for new information. People will begin respecting your opinion more when you voice it less.

2. Plant this thought in your mind and let it grow: "I really don't know everything. If I pay attention, maybe I can learn more than I know now and use this information to help identify a good solution." The truth is: You really *don't* know everything, no matter how expert you are in your field.

3. For three days, monitor your speaking time in all conversations and keep a written log of the following information: (1) who was present in your interactions; and (2) what proportion of time you held the floor. Many people spend a great deal more than their fair share of conversation time speaking or being the center of attention in the group, and do not realize that other people resent this, even from the "boss." Review your log. In interactions involving two people, each person should generally get about one-half the speaking time; in interactions with five people, each person would get roughly one-fifth the speaking time. If your speaking time is consistently greater than your fair share, set a personal goal for one month to keep quiet more, to listen, and to ask more questions of others. Force yourself to talk less.

Suggestions for Overcoming Aggressive Overconfidence

4. Identify someone you have been too aggressive with. Think of a specific incident when your words or actions were pushy and possibly hurtful to this person. Go back in your mind and see if you can restate your opinion less forcefully. *Write down* how you could have conveyed your message differently. Also write down a question or two you could have asked to draw the other person out and give them more speaking time. And how could you have disagreed with them, if you did, without blowing them away? Here's an example:

> *Liz, what's your revised timetable on the Avery project? (Liz says some unacceptable date, like August 18, but instead of berating her and stating a flat deadline of August 4, you say...) That's not really going to work. We need Tony to get the Elgin project initiated, and he can't be two places at once. How can we speed up the timetable or make some other arrangements?*

5. Go to the person, make yourself apologize for your previous action, and deliver your modified or corrected version of what you should have said. If it's too late to change the outcome entirely, simply apologize and explain that you are working on trying to do better in the future. And do so!

Notice how people react to you as you start making some of these positive changes. They are almost certain to enjoy you more and not dread seeing you coming.

Taking Mistakes in Stride

People with high self-confidence make just as many mistakes as anyone else; they just don't let these mistakes take over their attitude. When we fail, this gives us valuable information on what we can do differently. Failure becomes important feedback that helps us readjust our attitude and behavior. Remember: Good comes from a mistake. We learn things, and often unexpected positive things occur, too.

Instead of seeing a situation or person as a threat, treat it as a challenge or an opportunity. Did you ever wonder why some people are non-plussed by things that appear to be real obstacles for someone else? It's largely because they have adopted an attitude of "I will overcome." There is almost always some way around a barrier if we get creative. Don't hesitate to ask others for advice on a particularly sticky challenge.

We all have bad days when we slip into old habits of low confidence or pushiness, but a relapse is a time to rethink, grow, and learn. We are strengthened each time. Continue to be optimistic: think of setbacks as temporary. A setback will only be permanent if you give it permission to reside with you permanently! Leaders with high EQ take mistakes in stride.

CHAPTER 7

The Role of Self-Control in Emotional Intelligence

red was a division manager for a plastics corporation. He prided imself on his work ethic and his fairness to his employees. And it vas true: Fred's employees nearly always used the word "fair" to escribe him. And they used another word too: "distant" or "cold." Vhen Fred's father was dying of cancer, he didn't share this news vith anyone at work. He put on a stoic face and tried to concentrate n his job. People speculated about what might be wrong, because 'red seemed extra edgy and out of the office a lot. No one learned bout the situation until after his father's death. Said one employee, He would be a lot more human if he'd just let down a little bit."

·elf-control is based on our having a positive self-attitude and nough self-knowledge to make the right decision about what o do with an emotion. The thinking brain can make decisions bout emotions. Not all of them need to be expressed, but they lso don't need to be hidden or denied. Emotionally intelligent eople display feelings if they are relevant, and deal positively vith emotions they can't show. They show self-control at an ppropriate or balanced level and consistently are judged by thers to be less impatient, more willing to share ideas and isten to the ideas of others, less likely to be involved in conflict nd generally more likable. When we have the right amount of elf-control, we can also manage our own moods well.

Lack of Self-Control

There are two ways in which lack of emotional self-control can get us in trouble: (1) *not controlling our emotions enough,* either rom not knowing how to positively deal with them, or by not aring how these unguarded emotions infringe on or impact others: and (2) *over-controlling our emotions,* like Fred did in the opening example. Denying or ignoring emotions is equally problematic.

It is quite normal to feel some rage, some sadness, and some anxiety, just as it is normal to feel some love and some joy. For too many people, however, self-control means bottling up feelings, sentiments, and vulnerability, which other people assume is coldness, or an inability to feel and show emotion. This is perhaps the most misunderstood dimension of Emotional Intelligence in the workplace.

Many people have trouble with negative emotions, but failing to share with the people around you or even denying that you are angry, grieving a loss, or worried is not appropriate emotional control. Like it or not, we all experience these emotions; if we fail to express them and deal with them appropriately, they will return to haunt us in the form of physical complaints, poor health, moodiness, and ultimately lack of success in managing or interacting with other people.

The reality of human life is that we are always in some kind of mood and we are always receiving some kind of emotional data. We need to enjoy our feelings and learn from the ones we don't enjoy, without feeling that we must act on them or be frightened by them. They are simply a different form of data that comes to us as sensory and bodily impressions.

Whether we realize it or not, what we do in our free time (and even in some of our structured time) is manage our moods or emotions. We do this by making choices about who we spend time with, what we do, and where we spend our time. Learning to comfort or soothe ourselves is a fundamental life skill that most of us do automatically.

When a bad mood gets us in its grip and threatens to control us, we can admit the emotions to ourselves and those around us. Then we can take active steps to manage the mood.

1. Begin by observing how you act when you are in a bad mood. Relax and let yourself think about what works to get you out of the dumps: What things do you enjoy? Pick out at least three things you can give yourself or do for yourself to become motivated on a bad day. Write them down right here:

   _____

   _____

   _____

   Memorize these three and practice them faithfully.

2. Consciously plan some time each day for excitement, and some time for quiet. Too much excitement and pressure can leave us with the negative effects of stress, and too much quiet and calm can leave us feeling isolated and depressed. By making time for both, we feel more balanced, satisfied, and happy.

3. Develop a *Response Plan* (EQ Fundamentals) for challenging situations. Rather than letting these situations push your buttons, take control of your mood by envisioning each of the following situations right now, and plan how to positively handle each one:

   - a tough staff meeting
   - the annual meeting
   - confronting a subordinate
   - receiving your performance review
   - dealing with your least favorite colleague
   - meeting with a disgruntled client
   - another challenge you face

4. Take five to ten deep, cleansing breaths and let yourself get calmer when you feel any negative emotion building. This is very easy to do discreetly, even in a public place.

Suggestions for Managing Your Bad Moods

5. Change your environment. Move around and focus on something different for as little as 3 to 5 minutes.

6. Pay attention to the space where you work — it does affect your mood. Make it cheerful, with nice colors and some quiet mood music if you like. Turn up the lights: Research confirms that greater illumination increases energy. Create a pleasant and motivating environment for yourself with pictures and special objects that have meaning for you.

7. Eat a moderate amount of some nutritious food. You might be in need of additional brain fuel.

8. Do something completely different from what you're currently doing if you are feeling negative: listen to music, enjoy some hobby, engage in some form of art.

9. Keep something in your office that always makes you laugh. A laugh elevates your mood.

10. Focus on your relationships and engage in some fun activity.

11. If you can identify the source of your bad mood, brainstorm ways to actually begin to solve the problem. Ask yourself: "What steps can I take right now to make a positive difference?" There is generally at least one small thing you can do.

12. Plant positive thoughts, in your head, and remember to read over your *Positive Script*. (EQ Fundamentals, Chapter 4)

The Challenge of Anger

Anger, one of the most challenging emotions for most of us, is associated with our own history and memories of anger. The angry memory is immediately triggered in our emotional brains when we encounter something in the present that is even vaguely similar to some past event. Anger builds on itself: Once we are aroused by brain catecholamines (brain chemicals that produce energy), the arousal lasts for hours or even days. During this time, if we are provoked by something else, we react more strongly because we are already aroused. This partly explains why some people have more trouble controlling anger than any other emotion. Anger comes from feeling some sort of threat or danger to what we hold dear — even an idea or project. The limbic brain reacts immediately.

Suggestions for Dealing with Your Anger

Suppressing anger or letting it explode violently are proven health risks, and there are usually repercussions. Emotionally intelligent people have learned how to find a happy medium for dealing with anger.

1. Allow yourself to feel your anger, and don't bury or deny it. Activate your *Response Plan*. (Refer to Fundamentals, in Chapter 4 for details.)

2. *Reframe* (refer to Fundamentals) and look at the situation from a different perspective. Can it be interpreted differently?

3. Use all three parts of your brain by trying these suggestions:

   • Rational brain: Build your own logical arguments as to why you are justified. Write about it in your journal or write the person a letter that you *never* send.

   • Limbic brain: Let yourself truly feel the anger. Use moans, grumbles, and tears as you relive it in your head.

   • First brain: Be active — pace, shout, hit a pillow, do calisthenics — but do it privately.

4. Have a safe place where you can retreat and be alone. Engage in the activity that you have pre-planned. Can you exercise, play a game, watch a funny video, or read a funny or inspiring book?

Suggestions for Dealing with Your Anger

5. Allow yourself to brood in this way for a limited time only. Set a time limit appropriate for the offense and concentrate during that time on how awful it was. When that time is up, put the incident aside.

6. Use a *Programmed Relaxation Response* that you have practiced to calm you down when you feel stressed. (Details can be found in the Fundamentals section of Chapter 4.)

7. Take a "time out" by doing some kind of busy-work, like dusting the shelves in your office or filing papers.

8. Visualize a different, more agreeable possible outcome. As you visualize this, you will be taking the first step toward creating that outcome.

9. Focus on the things about the situation you *can* control and don't worry about the things you can't change.

10. Call a temporary truce with someone with whom you are having an ongoing battle. You can do this in a situation that is escalating by saying, "I'm feeling angry at this point, so let's take a break and get back together at (suggest a time). I think we can discuss it more calmly then." Then remove yourself and engage in one or more of the above suggestions.

11. If the angry encounter was with someone you have to deal with on a regular basis and you believe the left-over anger will get in the way of positive relations, ask for a conference to discuss the problem with the person. Do this only after you have had some cooling off time. When you meet, express your own anger to the other person in a non-blaming way. "I always get upset when the report is late because it's hard for me to do my job," rather than "You drive me crazy when you always get this information to me so late!" (To make sure such confrontations turn out positively, use the "Three-Step" in Fundamentals, in Chapter 4.)

What *Not* to Do with Anger

Research has shown that the folk wisdom in catharsis, getting out your anger by blowing up or attacking, is not helpful. In fact, venting is one of the worst ways to calm down, because physiologically, acting on anger produces more anger. If the other methods for reducing anger do not work, then, and only then, should you confront the person, but confront calmly and assertively, and only when you can control yourself.

Suggestions for Defending against Anger

Having to defend ourselves from someone else's anger can produce anger in us as well, especially if the attack is personal or extremely hostile. If you can stick it out and remain calm, the verbal attack will eventually subside. Emotionally intelligent people do not let others push their buttons: When the wrath subsides, focus on the other person in order to do one of the following:

1. Offer an apology, if one is needed.

2. Offer an explanation, if one is needed. However, if all you have is an excuse, then offer an apology.

3. Offer a solution. Think what you can really do to help improve the situation, and suggest it. Or ask, "What can *we* do about it?"

Suggestions for Receiving Criticism

It's hard for most of us to receive criticism or be the brunt of someone's anger without experiencing some hurt, anger, or embarrassment ourselves. If you have trouble controlling yourself in these circumstances, here are some ideas:

1. As you are getting attacked by another, tell yourself, "I can stand this. I did it before, and I can again. I am not the reason for the anger. I am okay. I am healthy. I will stay calm." Repeating positive phrases will help your rational brain stay in control of your emotions.

Suggestions for Receiving Criticism

2. Practice visualizing ahead of time if you think you will receive some criticism. See yourself turning on your Programmed Relaxation Response immediately afterward.

3. Resolve to learn something from the feedback. Remember that this is your opportunity to grow and become an even more fabulous person.

4. Remember to breathe slowly and deeply in order to remain calm.

5. Don't get defensive, get quiet. Make yourself *listen* fully.

6. Be honest about your feelings and reactions after the criticism. If you can't share them with the criticizer, write them later in your journal.

7. Summarize your understanding of what the other person said about you.

8. Show some willingness to change. Even if the critical person is exaggerating, they could have a point.

Worry

Another challenging emotion is worry. This emotion can play a useful function by helping us avoid danger and rehearse some solutions to difficult situations we might encounter. It helps us prepare. *If I worry about the sales report I have to make to the top brass, this will motivate me to be well-prepared.* The problem with worry, however, is that too much of it can cause panic attacks, phobias, or compulsive behavior. Chronic worry can be thought of as continuous, moderate-level arousal of the amygdala.

Suggestions for Reducing Worry

1. Increase self-awareness. Catch yourself just as you begin the chain of thoughts that leads to worry. If you are not sure what led you to worry, start paying attention to your thoughts and trace them back to what prompted them. Be aware of your body's responses, too.

2. The moment you catch yourself heading toward "worry," switch to your *Programmed Relaxation Response*. (EQ Fundamentals) Practice this when you are not worrying, too.

3. Engage in a reality check. Do some restructuring of your thinking. Ask yourself: How likely is it that the event will actually occur, on a scale of 1–10? What alternatives are there? What positive measures can I take to prevent it?

4. Do some contingency planning. Having a fall-back plan can help ease your worry because you will know what to do if "it" happens.

5. Plan distracting and pleasurable activities you can do when you catch yourself worrying. Get your mind off the worrisome event.

Sadness and Loss

We all experience some melancholy and despondency. Sadness is usually brought on by some form of loss or disappointment. The loss of anything familiar can be difficult: relationships, money, a job, dreams, projects, groups, youth, a loved one (separation, divorce, death), the old neighborhood, a pet, health, a routine, or anything that was important to us. Barring a serious depression that might require professional help, most of us can manage our own sadness if we learn how.

Make the most of sadness by learning from it. Do not let it overwhelm you. To deal with sadness, spend more time alone to reflect on and adjust to the loss. Just don't withdraw too far. While the natural inclination is to isolate yourself, the emotionally healthy person recognizes that this only makes things worse. Going over and over the sad thoughts doesn't help, either. So here are some helpful ideas:

Suggestions for Dealing with Sadness

1. Engage in your *Programmed Relaxation Response*. (EQ Fundamentals)

2. As with anger, develop a *Response Plan* (EQ Fundamentals) for what you will do when confronted with loss, and practice how to react.

3. Do something physical to get the blood flowing and increase the energy that has been sapped by the emotion of sadness.

4. Create a positive and motivating internal dialogue, a pep talk. "This is temporary and I will feel better soon. I know I can get through this." Challenge your sad thoughts with other alternatives. "I know I will find another job soon." "Yes, I can get along without her." "I know that I will make friends in this new town." Don't let the negatives keep going unchecked.

5. Focus on your goals and readjust them if needed. Perhaps this loss occurred in order to point you in another direction.

6. Ask someone for love and support. Turn to a trusted friend and confide the loss and your sadness.

7. Have a comforting ritual or routine: a certain meditative spot, a piece of comforting music, or a picture that lifts your spirits.

8. Have a special or inspiring memory about the person or thing you lost to hold onto.

9. Schedule pleasant and distracting activities. Go to a movie or some event that you normally enjoy. Read an inspiring book, or engage in some absorbing activity to get the good chemicals flowing again.

10. Allow yourself to be positively affected by nature or some form of beauty. Go to a peaceful and calming place.

Suggestions for Dealing with Sadness

11. Laughter is incompatible with sadness, so doing something that makes you laugh is guaranteed to drive away sadness temporarily and lift your spirits just a little. Keep funny books and video tapes around just for this purpose. Spend time with a funny friend.

12. Volunteer to do something to help someone else, or some non-profit organization you believe in. Doing something for someone who is even less fortunate than you is one of the most powerful ways to get your mind off your own problems.

> **Rule of thumb to remember:** When your limbic brain is aroused by anger or worry, do something to *calm* yourself down. When you are feeling lethargic (as with sadness), do something to *increase* your *energy* level. This is one of the A-B-Cs of mood control that all emotionally intelligent people practice.

Keeping Our Emotions in Balance

Self-control means balancing our emotions — not too little control of emotions, and not too much. When we are too much "in control" and stifle shows of emotion, usually it's because we think denial is the best way to handle emotional data, or because we assume that others will think negatively of us, or that emotions have no place in our lives. Such denial is unhealthy and unnatural. It *will* catch up with us and negatively impact our health. Suppressing our emotions takes a great deal of energy — energy that is then unavailable for other more useful purposes, like thinking and behaving.

Suggestions for Getting into Emotional Balance

If you want to remove those tight controls on your emotions, start building self-awareness (see Chapter 5), then move on to self-disclosure. Learn how to share more of what you think and feel. If you are sometimes accused of being cold or uncaring, try these suggestions:

1. Think of a thought or feeling you have that you might ordinarily keep to yourself. Try writing about it in your journal to make it more concrete. It need not be your deepest, darkest secret or most embarrassing moment, but make it something that you have trouble admitting.

2. Now think of someone — a spouse, a trusted friend, or a mentor that you know will not react in any negative way to your issue. Take a deep breath and tell the private thought you wrote about to your chosen person. Discuss it and allow yourself to become comfortable with having it out in the open. (It will get easier after the first sentence.) Continue to practice taking small risks like that with people you know you can trust. Not only will this result in better self-control but it will positively impact your relationships with others. Remember: Suppressing your emotions is the other extreme of letting them get out of control! Neither extreme is good.

3. Share a few personal activities from your private life with people at work. The manager who is willing to share a few things becomes more "human," and thus more respected. A good time to try this is at the beginning of your work week. Try telling someone a few sentences about what you did over the weekend.

4. Make yourself tell at least one trusted person at work about any personal struggle you may be experiencing (about, say, a sick family member or struggles with your teenager). While you need not share all the details, make yourself open up and be a little bit more human — and then watch how this improves productivity and relationships.

Maintaining a Positive Mood

When we are in the grip of a strong mood, we are less effective with the next challenge. Staying positive and on a relatively even keel is the key to fully utilizing our other cognitive and emotional abilities. Negative moods spread worse than viruses: If the boss is in a bad mood, *no one* is happy and, consequently, less work is getting done. (Maintaining an enthusiastic mood in the Social dimension will be covered more thoroughly in Chapter 9).

Stress

Part of self-control is dealing effectively with stress. We've known for many years about the negative effects of too much pressure, and the warnings are everywhere. Too much stress results in a lowered immune system, chronic diseases, reduced memory and cognitive ability, not to mention weakened relationships. Yet we still try to exceed our capacities.

The sources of stress can be external (the deadline) or internal (I "should" do such and such). Some of these sources of stress are within our control, and others are not. None of us can eliminate the stress that results from things we can't control, such as getting caught in a company downsize or experiencing the death of a loved one. We can choose, however, to take charge of those things that are under our control, and work to reduce the negative effects and cope better with those situations we can't control.

Studies clearly show that those who invest all their energy in one area show the effects of stress more readily. Having many interests in which we invest our time and commitment means that when something goes wrong in one area (which is inevitable), we can withstand the turbulence because we have other things from which we also derive pleasure and identity. Those who invest their identity in only one place, such as the organization, experience a much more severe blow to that identity during bad times. Downsizing, a failed project, or a "lateral transfer" can leave us with no sense of identity. Build balance in your life and take time for personal and leisure activities. You will have more energy and feel less overwhelmed when something goes wrong.

Suggestions for Coping Better with Stress

1. Stop the denial. Admit you are stressed and can't handle everything! Remain alert to times when you are losing energy or focus: These are signals that you need a change in your pattern of behavior.

2. Start believing that you are a changing and dynamic individual — as changeable as the world is. Staying flexible, rather than digging in your heels and refusing to change, is one important key to counteracting the negative effects of stress.

3. Set realistic goals. Pick what is really important, and let the rest of your "obligations" go.

4. Ask for help when you need it, and don't be afraid to say "no" to anything that doesn't fall in line with your priorities.

5. Get away from the office or from your main source of stress at least one day a week, *no matter what*.

6. Use your *Programmed Relaxation Response* (EQ Fundamentals) to calm you down.

7. Exercise. Rather than using up too much time, regular exercise will actually give you *more* time because it dramatically increases energy. Choose a physical activity you really enjoy, and start small.

Suggestions for Coping Better with Stress

8. At least three times a week, engage in one of several different activities that you enjoy and that calm you down. Any pleasurable hobby or pastime can fit the bill. Make this something very different from work to develop the other sides of yourself. If you are the accounting manager, managing the finances of your civic group is probably not going to be a stress reducer!

9. Get enough sleep. Let something else go, and get to bed earlier.

10. Read a good book on stress management, and practice what it says.

CHAPTER 8
The Role of Empathy in Emotional Intelligence

When Ed arrived at the office after his breakfast meeting, he noticed that his assistant Pat was sitting slouched at her desk. Always pleasant and cheerful and a diligent worker, she did not even look up when he came in, as if she wasn't aware of his arrival. Ed took one look and sensed that something was wrong. He proceeded to his office to put his things away, and then decided to go see what might be wrong. He went up to her desk and said kindly, "Hi, Pat. Is anything wrong?" She looked at him sadly and just shrugged her shoulders. He said, "I'll help you if I can. Would you like to come into my office and talk about it?" Pat hesitated a minute and then got up from her desk and followed Ed to his office.

Ed not only showed sensitivity to Pat, but also organizational wisdom: He understood that very little productive work would be accomplished unless he attended to her needs. Rather than ignoring her signals of distress, he decided to meet them head-on and use his own EQ to help Pat. Whatever the trouble, hearing an employee out for a few minutes and possibly being able to offer helpful suggestions is time well-invested because it builds trust and increases productivity over the long-term. We can help them deal with the problem and move on.

Success in social interactions is a hallmark of Emotional Intelligence. We need to develop the ability to accurately assess the other person or the group and respond accordingly. The first step toward skillful social behavior is social knowledge or awareness. Such awareness or ability to tune in to others and feel what they are feeling is called empathy. Without empathy, we have difficulty sustaining relationships. People with high EQ have a number of strong relationships in all areas of their lives.

As we concentrate on developing ourselves, we focus inward to improve our self-knowledge, attitude, and behavior. We improve our relationships, however, by focusing outward, to others — by paying careful attention to the other person instead of ourselves. We must observe carefully with our eyes, and listen with hypersensitive ears.

Developing the Ability to Empathize

One of the ways to become aware of the other person is to show empathy, the ability to understand another person's feelings by remembering a similar experience from our own life. We try to learn how and why they feel this way, and try to see things from their point of view. There can be no empathy without self-awareness of our own emotions, however, because we must *relate* to what they are going through on a personal level.

Not being able to recognize the feelings of others is a common and costly problem which lowers one's Emotional Intelligence. A manager needs empathy and the ability to know intuitively, in his or her gut, how others feel at times — managing employees, dealing with customers, leading change, and in virtually all the "people aspects" of getting the job done.

When someone starts to tell us about their situation, our limbic brain quickly searches its storehouse of memories for a time when we had a similar experience and felt the same way. Feeling it internally is just a start; we must also try to put a label on the feeling. The basic language of emotion works not only to describe our own emotions, but can also offer us the language for empathy.

As we explained in Chapter 2, research shows that our brains are hard-wired for empathy. As we get to know a person socially and professionally, and understand what they are feeling and why, it becomes easier to put ourselves in their shoes. That does not mean that we agree with everything they are thinking and feeling — just that we see things somewhat from their perspective. Empathy builds trust. Without trust, other people will not work collaboratively with us and we will have no power to influence them.

Suggestions for Becoming More Empathetic

1. Practice developing empathy skills by focusing on your most difficult employee. The *Walk-in-Their-Shoes* activity outlined in the Fundamentals section of Chapter 4 should help you understand what things are like for them.

2. Try to *"Look for Good/Look for Similar."* (See the Fundamentals section.) Always assume that people have the best of intentions. When they do have negative intentions, they will often be embarrassed into better behavior because others assumed better of them.

3. Keep a *Journal*. (See EQ Fundamentals.) As you write about your thoughts and experiences, add a couple of sentences, using feeling words. Start them off with "I felt…" Make yourself start to focus on emotions that are associated with certain experiences.

4. Observe and adopt a genuine attitude of curiosity and interest in the emotions of others. Reflect on and write about what emotions someone is likely to have had in certain situations. The more we can determine what another person's needs are by watching and by asking, the better position we will be in to help them. The more help we provide, the better ally they will be and the more willing to reciprocate.

5. As you identify a word or phrase that describes the emotion another person is showing try to reflect on an experience you have had that produced a similar emotion in you. What were your physical sensations? What was your body telling you? Learn to put an emotional label on this. While not everyone experiences exactly the same emotions in a particular situation, chances are good that the other person had similar feelings.

Suggestions for Becoming More Empathetic

6. Listen better. That means *don't talk* when someone else is sharing. Observe their non-verbal behavior carefully. (The next section will address this.)

7. Avoid distorted thinking: Do not overgeneralize or allow yourself to engage in thinking, "He never…" or "She always…." *Reframe* such thoughts. (EQ Fundamentals)

8. Use a *"Process" Comment* to find out what's really going on. (See Fundamentals.)

9. Ask trusted others for feedback on how well you are projecting empathy.

Reading Social Cues: Listening with Our Eyes

Empathy also comes when we more accurately read non-verbal cues such as posture, facial expression, and tone of voice. Non-verbal cues include everything about communication except the words. Researchers tell us that about 90% of a given message is contained in the non-verbal cues while only about 10% of the meaning is contained in the words. Smooth communication requires us to pay attention to more than just the words, yet this is not what we do.

The physical reactions that accompany words are automatic responses that are directly linked to emotions. When you attend to non-verbal cues, look for physiological changes which show up in facial muscles, posture, gestures, voice pitch, volume or word emphasis, the color of the face or neck, and the breathing rate. All these signs are visible if we train ourselves to pay attention. Rather than focusing inward and rehearsing what we want to say, we should tune in to these cues so we can better understand how we should react. **When non-verbal cues indicate one thing and the words say something else, believe the non-verbals!**

People who are adept at reading these cues are better adjusted socially and considered by others to be more socially competent. Social awareness greatly aids success in leadership

oles. With practice, we can all improve — and this will
improve our chances of success. The following table can serve
as a guideline for interpreting the subtle cues other people
present to us.

Part of Body	Behavior of the Speaker	Probable Meaning
1) EYES	Does he/she meet our eyes?	Confident, willing, honest
	Do they look down?	Sad, worried, guilty, depressed, or dishonest
	Do they look away, to the side?	Concerned about something "out there," or in a hurry
2) FACE	Is the face tight, narrowed?	Angry, worried, or pressured
	Is the face loose, relaxed?	Content, pleased, relaxed
3) MOUTH	Is the mouth set in a straight line?	Serious, concentrating (if tightly set)
	Is the mouth turned down?	Sad, depressed
	Is the mouth upturned?	Happy, enthusiastic
4) SHOULDERS	Shoulders held high and forward?	Tense, angry, worried, anxious, hurried
	Shoulders held high and back?	Proud, ready to go
	Shoulders drooping forward?	Discouraged, depressed
5) POSTURE/ POSITION	Facing listener squarely, with open posture?	Confident, serious, paying attention
	Facing to the side or closed?	Disinterested or unaccepting of what's being said
6) HAND GESTURES	Fist clinched?	Angry, stressed
	Hands flying wildly around?	Excitement or trying to get attention
7) COLOR OF FACE	Flushed with red?	Angry, embarrassed, excited
	Drained of all color?	Afraid, disbelieving, horrified

Be alert for any changes: They will tell you that the person's emotions have shifted, which might require you to shift your own behavior (see Chapter 10).

Tone of Voice

A person's tone of voice provides important clues about the meaning of the message. Most of us understand what all the nuances mean: louder-than-normal tone indicates anger or stress, while soft tone, especially with rising intonation at the end of sentences, suggests uncertainty and questions. A soft tone accompanied by other signs of anger (physical tension, glaring eyes, etc.) suggests that the person is trying to stay in control. Rapid speech indicates excitement, and slow speech indicates worry, fatigue, or depression.

We know these things; the problem is that we don't pay attention to them. We minimize their importance because it is easier to respond to the words if we take them at face value. We might be busy ourselves or preoccupied about what we want to say next, or just not interested in what the other person has to say. So we pay attention only to their words, rather than where the true message lies — in their tone of voice or body language.

Once we get to know an employee or co-worker, it is easy enough to pick up on subtle changes in tone of voice. This is critical, in fact, if we are to be effective in the Social dimension. A voice tone of worry or anger, for example, should be a wake-up call to the leader to ask more questions or try to offer help. These emotions do not go away, and if ignored by the manager, they will invariably return in a stronger form, which will probably be much more disruptive. Dealing with people's emotions in the early stages will allow office relationships to run more smoothly.

Listening — The Vehicle to Empathy

Most of us are not nearly as good at listening as we think we are. The true proof of our listening ability is not how we rate ourselves, but how others we interact with regularly rate how well we listen. Ask colleagues how good a listener you are, and be ready for a surprise.

We all have certain things we are predisposed to hear, and a habit of not hearing certain other things. We don't hear what a certain person said because we don't like him or her and aren't really interested, or we hear only facts because we think everything else is a waste. Yet good listening skills are the keys to genuine empathy: When we practice selective listening, we cut ourselves off from important sources of data, and risk alienating other people. When we learn to listen better we gain the additional data we need to become a good leader and earn the respect of those we work with.

Suggestions for Improving Listening Effectiveness

1. Train your mind to listen. Approach the speaker with the *intention* of listening. If this is truly an impossible time to listen, be honest with the speaker and make an appointment for another time when you can sit down together for a discussion.

2. Focus your attention completely on the other person. Put down the pen and the telephone, and move away from the computer. Give the person who is talking your undivided attention. Don't even worry about what you will say; just listen. This is not the time to focus on yourself. If you take those few extra minutes right now to really listen, the person won't have to keep coming back to try to get your attention.

3. Maintain eye contact throughout the interaction.

4. Say nothing. Be quiet and let the other person talk. Let them say what they want to say. When you are listening, *most of the words should be theirs, not yours.* Allow enough time to let the person speak, without jumping right in with your own comments the minute they take a breath.

Suggestions for Improving Listening Effectiveness

5. Let the person know you are listening: Nod or occasionally say "uh-huh." Summarize or paraphrase the content of what he or she said. Repeat back what they said in your own words ("In other words..." "So basically, what happened was...").

6. While the speaker is talking, quickly and silently recall a time in your own experience when you were in a similar position. Perhaps you did not feel exactly like what the person speaking to you is feeling, but when you put yourself in their shoes, you can see where they are coming from.

7. Attach a label to their feelings. Try this: "You seem pretty upset about the change," or "I can tell you are feeling a lot of pressure to do a good job with this project." You might not have labeled their feelings accurately, but they will correct you. The point is that the other person will keep talking and release their tension.

8. Ask open-ended questions to enhance your understanding of the situation; they give you more information. Use questions that begin with *how*, *what*, or *why?*

9. The speaker's own thoughts, feelings, and actions become clear as they give voice to their feelings. The listener does not have to say or do much. Do not be quick to jump in with answers, just allow the person to figure it out on their own whenever possible. This is empowerment — letting them figure it out. You may prompt them to become solution-oriented by asking. "What do you think you should do now?"

What To Do When Listening

We all know people who can't wait to tell a long and involved story about when *they* were in a similar situation. This is the last thing the speaker wants to hear! When you tell the other about *your* situation and what *you* did about it, this takes the focus off the speaker's problem and puts it back on you, the manager. This is arrogant and insensitive. A little self-disclosure might be helpful in this particular situation, but make *sure you do not offer more than a sentence or two*. Then bring the conversation back to the speaker's situation: "I had something similar on my last job, and I got pretty upset about it until we worked out the details. So I can understand why you are upset now."

Why Empathy Is So Vital

Dealing with an emotional situation as it presents itself is an important way to put out a small fire before it becomes a conflagration and begins to consume or destroy morale. Employees do not always come knocking on the manager's door asking to talk! That's why we have to be aware of these clues whenever we notice them and respond with empathy. This will prevent bigger problems later.

Empathy is not just for problems, however. Discussing things at work that have nothing to do with work, such as children, hobbies, or the arts, provides the emotionally intelligent leader with information about co-workers. These social interactions tell us what is important to other people. We can use this genuine empathy we've been working on to build good work relationships. Empathy increases trust and closeness, enables work processes and tasks to flow more freely, and improves our enjoyment and our productivity. If you ask Don how his son's baseball team is doing and say, "I know you're proud of him," the next time you need information or assistance from Don or anyone in Don's department, you are more likely to get it.

CHAPTER 9

Motivation and Emotional Intelligence

Molly, the Vice President of HR, was handed a daunting assignment — to take a long, hard look at the company's problems with employee turnover. Her CEO wanted a full report, with recommendations, in 60 days. Three weeks had already gone by, and Molly was clearly avoiding the project. She was overwhelmed and had no idea where to begin. The issue of employee turnover hit home: she'd taken a recent call from a headhunter herself, and although she turned him down, the call had stimulated her thinking. Molly was feeling tired and drained at work, unable to muster motivation for much more than her day-to-day activities.

Emotion is the foundation for creativity, passion, optimism, drive, and transformation. *Motivation* is a synonym for enthusiasm, initiative, and persistence. A positive attitude in the Social dimension is motivation, one of the key facets of Emotional Intelligence and of leadership.

A thought without emotion falls flat; it is emotion attached to the thought that acts as the springboard, the energy that's needed for action. Without emotions, whatever work we do likely would be done robotically, thus affecting the entire organization, including business relationships. Motivation — internal energy that moves outward in one direction — is a quality that distinguishes the good leader from the great one. But where does such motivation come from?

The Importance of Meaning

It is important that we attach meaning to what we do, because without it, it will be very difficult to sustain our motivation or energy. When was the last time you asked yourself the real purpose of your job? Beyond meeting this year's sales goals, that is, or cutting the budget by another 10% or reaching gross revenues of $50 million or scoring a personal financial coup. *What does it all mean?* A leader who is not committed to the organization's purpose and who does not genuinely believe that the purpose is somehow meaningful to society will never be able to inspire others.

Motivation is not a something "out there" that pushes us. We feel external pressure when others urge us to do, be, or achieve something, but allowing our lives to be shaped by externals depletes our creativity and our energy, and is hard to sustain in the long-term. Motivation is based on a very deep level of what we truly want — an internal force that we can then focus toward the outside world. People who lack enthusiasm have allowed themselves to get so caught up in externals that they have lost touch with that internal fire. We can do most things that we really *want* to do! When we understand our purpose and see that it gives our lives meaning, we are motivated and strengthened with an internally guided commitment that overshadows external pressure. Motivation keeps the fires going!

Defining Your Purpose

When was the last time you actually spent quality, reflective time thinking deeply about what you really want? Most of us get so caught up in details and activities that we lose touch with all our passion. Passion comes from the emotional brain, and when we lose touch with our deepest desires — our passions — we cut off our feelings and jeopardize our health. If our activity isn't guided by our deep desires, we will not be able to muster up the motivation to pursue that activity. If we ignore what we deeply desire for our lives, we are, in a sense, being untrue to ourselves. Failing to recognize who we really are inside will prevent us from acquiring Emotional Intelligence, jeopardize our physical health (the body-mind connection), and worst of all — keep us from attaining true happiness.

When we are feeling genuinely satisfied with our lives, we are probably on the right path. Satisfaction is just a milder form of passion or motivation. We need the respite that satisfaction brings because we cannot sustain intense motivation indefinitely without resting and regrouping. Even in our less passionate moments, the intensity of meaning and purpose is still evident within us and serves to guide our actions.

Reconnecting with your purpose is a great way to restore energy and motivation to your life. How badly do you *want* something? Are you *motivated*? If you do not have much enthusiasm, then you have not tapped into that internal source of meaning — what you really enjoy and what's really most important to you. *This* is what will get you enthusiastic and motivated. Dig in your heart to find that spark of energy that will light *your* internal fire.

Suggestions for Finding Meaning in What You Do

1. Keep a *Journal*. (See details in Fundamentals, Chapter 4.)

2. If you have trouble clearly articulating exactly what you want, let yourself think, meditate, relax, and *feel* what moves inside you. Anything you really want will be felt in your gut. Think it and say it, and do not allow your cognitive brain to bury your desire with the attitude, "Why want it when I can't have it?" If you can't do it as a career, find a way to do it as an avocation.

3. Pay attention to what excites you, and then do more of it! Give yourself permission and opportunity to fall in love with an idea, an object, a project, a person, work, leisure, or anything else that brings out the best in you. This is an important key to emotional well-being. Everyone needs at least one area of life in which they feel enthusiasm.

4. Think about things from the past that have "turned you on." What elements of those things can you re-create in the present?

5. Use *"Process" Comments* (explained in Fundamentals) with another person. This will help you reestablish meaning in an ongoing relationship.

Suggestions for Finding Meaning in What You Do

6. Look at your organization with fresh eyes. Pretend you are telling a 6 year old about what you do. They don't want to know the details; they want to know how what you do affects them and how it affects other people. (Not *we make brake assemblies*; but *we make the brakes for your bike that help stop you from running out into the street and getting hit by a car.* Not *we manage health care systems*; but *we take care of the money for the hospitals so they can help people get well.*

    Describe the meaning of your job in the words of a child. How does what you do help people or help make the world a better place? Write it here:

    _____

    _____

7. If you need professional help to do this, then go get it. There is nothing like personal or career counseling to help you get things straight and find your path. Until you take the necessary steps, you will not be able to muster much enthusiasm for anything.

Optimism

A person with a positive attitude is a pleasure to be around. In fact, we gravitate toward such people, and their optimism tends to be infectious! Optimists pull more customers their way, and people who work for optimists are more productive: We work harder to please optimistic co-workers, customers, subordinates, and superiors and we enjoy working with them. No one wants to spend much time with someone who is sarcastic or surly, or who always sees the negative in everything! Optimists are more successful in creating whatever results they are seeking.

Optimism is associated with hope, and *hope* is a good predictor of success on a difficult job. Hope or optimism, an important part of Emotional Intelligence, allows us to carry on despite the inevitable obstacles we will encounter. Those with less Emotional Intelligence (and less hope, in particular) give up easily when they encounter difficulties. People with an optimistic attitude see failure as temporary. It is something that can be changed, and they have some control over the circumstances of the failure. Pessimists often see failure as part of some personal characteristic that is permanent and unchangeable. They also look for what is bad in the external world, ignoring what is good.

Psychologists tell us that the feeling of hopelessness can lead to depression, with its resulting lack of energy and motivation. We must convince ourselves that mistakes are only permanent if we let them be permanent. Perhaps we cannot completely erase a mistake or control all the external factors, but we *can* find a way not to let a mistake completely block our path. We can reduce errors and obstacles by concentrating on those things we can control. The only thing we can control and change 100% of the time is our attitude: If we think the world stinks, we will find plenty of evidence to support this notion, and that will surely justify our hopeless and pessimistic attitude! An emotionally intelligent person looks for the good in the world, in the community, and in the workplace (and finds plenty of that). It's just a matter of shifting our perspective, and using more of the space in our thinking and emotional brains to hold on to the good stuff!

Suggestions for Increasing Motivation and Optimism

Where do you get motivation when you have none, like Molly at the beginning of the chapter? Where do you get a positive attitude when the world looks bleak? If you are filled with lethargy, fear, depression, or frustration, you should seriously consider professional help. Here are some things you can also do to help yourself:

1. Use a *Journal* to express thoughts about your own purpose or calling. What comes naturally to you? Is this what you are currently doing, or do you need to make some changes?

Suggestions for Increasing Motivation and Optimism

2. Focus on your own internal voice — your dialogue with yourself. If yours says things like, "I'll never get this done," or "They won't like it, I know they won't," consciously and deliberately reprogram it for positive thoughts. Use your *Positive Script:* "I've done a good job before, and I can certainly do this." (See Fundamentals.)

3. If your dialog says something like "This whole place stinks," then it's time to make a change. What is it you really want, and where do you want to be? Consider a job change.

4. Each day on your way to work, have a talk with yourself — a pep talk. Tell yourself "I can get done today all that I need to do," or "This is going to be a good day." Repeat your affirmation over and over again.

5. At the end of the day, list five good things that happened that day. Even on bad days, you can think of a few things that went well — even inconsequential things. This will help you adopt the attitude that things are never completely bad.

6. List the projects you are involved in at work and how they are relevant to your meaning and calling in life. If you have almost nothing in your job that is meaningful, how can you get more work that really means something to you? Discuss possible new directions with your own manager.

7. Imagine that this is your Best Day Ever. You're getting a great deal accomplished, and energy is flowing. Tap into the enthusiasm you would feel on such a day.

8. Set aside a Focus Time each day or each week (such as 20 minutes daily or 2 hours each week). Shut your door, hold your calls, alert your staff that you are unavailable, and work on important concentrated work. Schedule this time in your planner; keep a running list ahead of time of projects or tasks to be done during your Focus Time. Small successes on big projects help keep your motivation up for the long haul.

Suggestions for Increasing Motivation and Optimism

9. Consider the size of the task. Any large project can be broken down into steps that are manageable. Begin by making a list of the steps. If you make the first step a relatively easy one, you'll be sure to be able to take the next step. Success adds immeasurably to motivation.

10. Create a Personal Motivation Team. Think now of three to five people you can count on — people you trust who make you feel good and who can generally lift your spirits. They should be people who inspire you. Have a frank and honest discussion with these people and let them know that you are trying to do some future planning. Ask them if they would be willing to serve on your Personal Motivation Team, to be called on as needed. Offer to reciprocate and do the same thing for them.

11. Look for a model to emulate. Better still, look to several people you admire for their level of motivation and their general ability to lead. If you know them well enough, you might want to ask them for advice, or even ask them to serve as your mentor. Find out what keeps them going through tough times.

Creativity

As we work on discovering and increasing our internal motivation, we often find that we can begin to approach things with fresh eyes and fresh ideas. Enthusiasm helps to spark creativity. Excellent leaders with high EQ are always on the lookout to make things better, and so add value to the organization. Without motivation, creativity, and flexible thinking, the value of our contributions is limited. We need to learn to value and encourage new ideas in ourselves and others, suspend negative judgments, and be advocates of such ideas. This involves giving people permission to *think outside the box* by removing barriers, so that the energy or motivation of our employees can take over.

Suggestions for Increasing Creativity

1. Remain open to ideas. Be slow to criticize, and *never* say immediately that an idea will not work, no matter how crazy it seems.

2. Really *listen* to the suggestions and ideas of others. Do not assume that you have all the answers or that the current modis operandi is the only way.

3. Get the presenter of the idea to give you more information, mull it over, and get others to look at the ideas, too. What parts of the idea look workable, even if the idea cannot be adopted in its entirety?

4. Encourage people to work together, because good ideas often emerge from collaboration.

5. Engage in structured brainstorming sessions with trained facilitators or with someone on your staff who knows or can learn this skill. Push for quantity of ideas — even outlandish ones.

6. Use "Process" Comments to challenge a group that might be stuck. Process comments are observations about what lies behind certain actions or comments. Get to the reasons why.

7. Reward and recognize people for contributions they make. Never take credit for the ideas of another, and always recognize and reward good ideas. Those that are implemented should receive some tangible reward.

8. Read outside your field of expertise and look for ways to connect the information to your job or work.

The Power of Difficulties

When we are troubled by the loss of a job or a loved one, for example, we are thrown off balance and lose motivation or even interest in our work. This adjustment period is normal and should even be expected. (See Chapter 7 on Self-Control.) However, out of these difficult times come windows of opportunity, when we begin to take stock of our lives and make what changes we can to better prepare for the bumps that lie ahead, as well as the new opportunities. The body, mind, and emotions regain strength, motivation returns, and we re-enter life with renewed zeal. Reframe the challenges you encounter as opportunities to take stock, re-adjust, and make another positive assault on life. It's all in the attitude.

CHAPTER 10

Social Competency and Emotional Intelligence

Ted walked up to a group of three colleagues who were laughing and talking about a movie two of them had seen over the weekend. They were telling their other co-worker, Barbara, about some of the funny parts. Ted listened for a few seconds, and said "Hey, you wanna know what I did this weekend? I went to a roller derby. Now <u>that</u> was funny." The others just nodded their heads at Ted and soon went their separate ways.

You probably know someone like Ted who has poor social skills or a poor sense of timing. Such people often leave a trail of unsuccessful relationships behind them, and never quite seem to get it together. Effective leadership and success in business depends in part on being able to develop deep and lasting relationships, as well as relationships that are social and short-lived. You must be able to engage in pleasant office chit-chat with colleagues and customers and get along with others.

People will usually give us clues as to what to say in order to connect with them. If we observe and listen carefully, we can pick up valuable information that will help us bridge the gaps that exist between us and them. Social skills build on the EQ factors previously discussed: self confidence, empathy, and an optimistic attitude toward others. Mastering these areas will set the stage for appropriate social behavior.

Appropriate behavior in the Social dimension leads to Social Competency. To develop such social skills, we must focus on other people, rather than on what we are experiencing or want to say. If we are preoccupied, we will not be able to pay close enough attention to the other person in order to know how to respond appropriately. And that will soon become obvious.

Levels of Relationships

Understanding the levels of intensity in relationships can help provide a framework for developing social skills. Relationships build in intensity in four general levels, but many relationships span more than one level. These 'steps' are as follows:

1) **Social pleasantries:** This first level covers behaviors and words that acknowledge another person, such as smiles, nods, and greetings, like "How are you?" We interact on this level when we see someone in the hallway or on the street. Sometimes it ends there, and sometimes we move on to another level.

2) **Facts:** This level of interaction is characterized by a sharing of demographic or public information about ourselves or our work, such as our name, where we live, where we are from, where we work, whether we have a family, and even "Yes, I'm currently involved in a project investigating Internet fraud." I provide you with some information, and you provide me with some. This level involves an information-exchange and professional-meeting/cocktail-party kind of talk.

3) **Thoughts and ideas:** When we get to know others better or work with them closely, we share our thoughts, opinions, and suggestions. When we move to this level, we are ready to invest more of ourselves, and we are more susceptible to criticism and conflict. Others might embrace our thoughts and ideas, or reject us if their own perspective differs sharply from ours. Many business interchanges take place at this stage. Typical comments at this level are: "I think we should…" or "I agree with Terry."

4) **Feelings:** This is our deepest and most vulnerable level — the emotional level, where we share the real feelings behind our opinions and ideas. This level often moves people most powerfully because they can connect at the most basic and universal human level. This is the level of collaborative relationships. True leaders are willing to move to this level. Using self-disclosure is a good way to get there. People seldom come out and say "I'm really worried about…," so the leader will also have to pay close

attention to tone of voice, body language, and shifts in behavior, then draw people out and be willing to share his or her own feelings.

Emotionally intelligent people know which level is appropriate in which circumstances. They also know that interactions proceed more smoothly when we are on the same level with another person. Refusing to move to another level with someone and moving too quickly can each derail a relationship. Socially competent people are those who can and often do move others through to Level 4, because it is only at this level that we truly connect *with* another person. People who are good at bringing other people to their mood, zeroing in on the mood of another person, adjusting to various levels of interactions, and moving relationships to deeper levels have smoother interpersonal interactions. This is an important EQ skill.

Basic Social Skills

General social competency also includes those little rules of social interaction we call *social skills*. When we are weak in any of them, we don't seem to "fit in." In this case, how can we possibly handle a department full of employees or lead people? Weak social skills make others feel uncomfortable and will limit our success. Fortunately, we can improve our social skills and learn how to get along in a group. Seek out the help of a coach, a mentor, or a therapist; the effort will be worth it. And help yourself, too, by learning the rules below.

"The Rules" of Social Interactions

1. **Acknowledge others.** Always say hello or acknowledge with a nod or a wave *anyone* who speaks to you. (In fact, try to speak to them first!) Never pass someone without smiling or otherwise acknowledging their presence; rudeness has no place in the organization, and will certainly get you nowhere fast.

"The Rules" of Social Interactions

2. **Initiate conversation.** Make yourself speak to any person you do not know who is seated or standing near you at an event. Don't wait for others to speak first; just take a deep breath and greet them. Share a few facts about yourself and ask the other person about themselves. Practice until you become comfortable doing this.

3. **Keep a conversation going.** Try to find something that interests you about the other person, and comment on that. "Oh, you live in Chapel Hill? I went to school at UNC." You don't have to like the whole person (and often won't), but you can find one thing to appreciate. Observe the other person and focus on every detail with curiosity, but suspend judgment. Observing them will give you clues about who they are, and give you good practice in improving social skills.

4. **Pace.** Pacing refers to the act of mirroring the non-verbal cues of the other person, as well as their general emotional state. It is based on empathy — the ability to mimic internally the feelings of another. Allow your body and your face to show interest and reflect emotion appropriate to what is being discussed. Synchronous non-verbal behaviors such as doing what the other is doing or leaning and smiling make it easier to share emotions and allow you to pick up on what others are feeling.

    Don't "pace" with another for your own gain. This is manipulation, and people *always* see through someone who is not genuine. Genuine concern for the other person and a desire to connect with them is necessary if you are to build good relationships. Pacing also allows us to be accepted and included in a group. Ted, the guy at the beginning of the chapter who broke up a group of kibbutzing colleagues by taking over "their" discussion, could have used this method.

5. **Backtrack.** Backtracking is a way to acknowledge a person before you lead a conversation in another

"The Rules" of Social Interactions

direction. You can do this more successfully if you summarize with a sentence or two what you believe the other person has just said so they will know you are "with" them. They will then be more willing to change the subject and discuss your issue. For example, if your two colleagues are talking about the Monday night football game and you want to discuss a project with one of them, make a few comments about the game or ask a question if you didn't see it. Then say, "Gil, I needed to talk to you about the task force agenda." Gil is more likely to move to your topic when you have acknowledged the importance of his. Pacing and backtracking in order to connect with another person's thought makes them more open to your opinions and feelings. It is the basis of persuasion and influence.

6. **Enter a conversation correctly.** Timing is critical in social interactions. *Never* interrupt another person in order to enter a conversation: People resent pushiness in conversation and will often ignore what you say. Listen for a few minutes first and use your body language to pace. Someone will usually acknowledge your presence by looking at you. You can also wait for a pause in an ongoing conversation, but be sure to ask a question or offer a comment about what the others were saying before you begin to take the conversation where you want it to go. (This is backtracking.)

7. **Reciprocity.** Reciprocity, another valuable social skill, has to do with putting the same amount of time or energy into a relationship that the other person is putting in. We have all known people who like us more than we like them or people who do not return our feelings. Relationships that are not on similar intensity levels (where both parties contribute equally and act on the same level) cannot survive. If you have to work with or relate regularly to someone, be sure you contribute an equal amount to the relationship. If you do not know how intensely they view the relationship, look for clues in their body language and behavior.

"The Rules" of Social Interactions

8. **Bring others to your mood.** If you want to bring others
to your mood or your preferred relationship level first
show empathy and pace with them. Self-disclosure is
also helpful, because when you reveal your own
preferences and feelings, you will move others and help
them to see your perspective, even if they do not fully
agree with you. Skilled leaders know that they
sometimes have to share their own thoughts and feelings
before they ask others to do so. When they open up,
others are far more willing to collaborate and be
persuaded.

Here are a few other social do's and don'ts relating to
Emotional Intelligence.

- Know when to laugh: Laugh when others laugh, but never
laugh at the expense of a marginalized group. And don't
laugh at another person unless they are laughing at
themselves, as well.
- Know what questions to ask, and never ask a question that
you are not willing to answer yourself.
- Understand personal space. Cultures view the acceptable
physical space between two people quite differently; know
what the culture preferences are for your colleagues, but
there are some general rules: If people back up from you,
you are standing too close; if people try to get closer to you,
the distance between you is uncomfortable. Be willing to
stand either a little closer than you would prefer or a little
further away than you would like if you sense that someone
is moving around a lot.
- Take turns in a conversation. A conversation is not a
monologue, so do not take more than your share of the talk-
time. On the other hand, if you seldom speak up, talk a little
more. People tend to mistrust the person who never talks.
- When in doubt, don't say it. If you are not sure how a
remark or question will be interpreted, don't voice it.

Suggestions for Developing Social Skills

1. Use a *Mind Video* of yourself succeeding at an upcoming social gathering. (EQ Fundamentals, Chapter 4)

2. Go to a social, civic, or professional event. If you are somewhat reserved, resolve to meet at least three people. Practice moving them to at least Level 3 in the interaction, using more self-disclosure than you are usually comfortable with.

3. Take every opportunity to practice initiating conversations and pacing with others. Introduce yourself to the person seated next to you on the airplane. Even if you are both working, three minutes of pleasant conversation is good practice.

4. Remind yourself to *Look for Similar / Look for Good*. (EQ Fundamentals, Chapter 4) Find the areas of commonality so real communication can begin.

5. When you begin to prepare for your next presentation or meeting in which you intend to advance your point of view, plan to do more than present facts: Be persuasive. Decide ahead of time what you will say that is beyond your usual. Offer your thoughts and ideas and express your attitude, your passion, your motives — in short, your emotions. Explain why you believe something or why it is personally meaningful to do it this way; this tactic is nearly always successful when we are trying to persuade others to adopt our point of view.

6. Get your mentor or coach to practice going to Level 4 with you. Work on becoming more comfortable discussing your feelings.

Suggestions for Developing Deeper Relationships

Once we learn these basics, we can begin to deepen a relationship. Every one of us benefits from having a number of relationships that have the *capacity* to reach into Level 4 when the need arises, and some relationships should be there on a regular basis. Cooperation, morale, and productivity will rise in the office to the extent that we are able to deepen our working relationships. Try the following to move from superficial relationships to deeper ones:

Suggestions for Developing Deeper Relationships

1. Use more self-disclosure. Share how you really feel about an issue and why you feel that way. Share not just from the head but from the heart; say it with conviction. Reveal some of your worries and concerns. This will show your "human" side and encourage the other person to respond in kind.

2. Keep a log of what levels of encounter you had with others during the day. As you become familiar with your current level of interaction with a specific person, try going one level further in the next interaction. Record the reactions.

3. Invite another person to come to Level 4 with you. Try it this way; "You told me what you think, Linda. But I want to know how you *really feel* about this. *"Process Comments"* (EQ Fundamentals) are particularly effective in deepening a relationship.

4. If the person is still reluctant to move to a deeper level with you even when invited, don't push it. Stay in Levels 1–3 with them for a while, but resolve to try again later. Some people are slower than others in allowing themselves to become vulnerable. Respect that, but don't give up on it if this is someone you relate with on a regular basis. Work on building the level of trust.

5. Identify a particular relationship that you might be able to deepen. Record in a *Journal* any thoughts about a possible conversation in which you share your feelings about something you are working on. Go to the other person and discuss the issue by revealing your feelings.

6. Keep confidences. Trust takes a long time to build, but it can be shattered in an instant.

Suggestions for Developing Deeper Relationships

7. Keep your promises. Say what you will do, and always do what you say — or offer a prompt and reasonable explanation why you didn't.

8. Listen actively, and talk less.

Persuasion and Influence

When we express our opinions and feelings about an issue, we are engaging in persuasion. Persuasion involves more than simply advancing logical arguments: People who are persuasive offer their passions and emotions along with their thoughts. We've all been exposed to highly persuasive people who can move us. They appeal to our emotional brains and to common human experiences; we describe them as *impassioned* and it is their passion that sets them apart.

A great leader influences others for mutual gain, and not just for personal advantage. We can more easily influence or lead people when we convince them that we are genuinely interested in them. That's one reason why empathy and all the other social skills we have described are so important. Persuasion and the ability to advance our point of view is a vital leadership skill, as well, reflecting a high degree of EQ.

Persuasion, NOT Manipulation

We have all met charming people who turn out to be manipulative. The charmer often possesses considerable social skills, but is a social chameleon who tries to be all things to all people in an effort to get ahead. The emotionally intelligent individual, by contrast, is one who might try to persuade another person to a certain end, but refuses to compromise his or her integrity and identity to do so. If you passionately state your case, or why your product or service is best, or why your project deserves to be funded, you are more likely to persuade someone than if you deliver a cold, dispassionate accounting of the facts or deliver a slick political appeal that says only what the audience wants to hear. Emotionally intelligent people know where the "manipulation" boundaries are, and refuse to cross them.

Encountering a New Situation

It is normal to feel a little nervous in a new situation. Let's take the example of a new job. Even people who seem self-assured experience a little anxiety, because we don't know what to expect and we all want to "fit in" when we go to a new job. The best way to do this is to try to move with the rhythm of the office: If everyone stands around the coffee maker in the mornings and engages in chit-chat, do this yourself — even if you aren't a coffee drinker! If "the group" goes to lunch together, go with them. Try going to lunch with a different person or group each day in order to get to know them. Enter into their routine for at least two weeks, until you meet people and become known. Here are some additional suggestions:

Suggestions for the New Job

- When you start a new managerial job, plan to spend your first several months simply listening and learning. Never come in as a new person with a preconceived idea of what's needed, or armed with a list of changes that you lay out in the course of your first week. If you move too quickly before you have collected enough data and built trust, you will spend a great deal of time trying to make corrections later and persuading people to get on board.

- The best way to build trust is by going out and meeting the people who *do* the tasks that you are managing. Follow them around in order to learn about the situations they encounter, and listen, listen, listen. Never be critical at this stage; just try to genuinely learn. Ask for their opinions and suggestions. The implementation phase of any change will be shorter if you have done this, because people will "buy in" and support you. Spend plenty of time in the exploration and planning stage before you implement a change.

Suggestions for the New Job

- Make one friend you can depend on to show you the ropes. This can be a boss or a peer, or even a long-timer who works for you. Don't hesitate to ask this person for what you need; it's better to ask and show an interest in learning their ways than it is to blunder ahead and make a faux pas. You don't want to lose your forward momentum in the office.

- Get to know all the resources you have at your disposal. Spend a little time one-on-one with each of your employees and peers, mostly asking questions and listening to them. Look for a strength in each employee that you can use as you move ahead.

CHAPTER 11

Promoting Emotional Intelligence in Others: Developing an Employee

Peter was in a hurry to catch a plane. He went flying into Becky's office, knowing she was out of the office for the afternoon. He dropped a pile of papers with a hastily scrawled post-it note saying "Friday" on her chair, where she could not miss them. He was sure she knew what corrections he needed on the spreadsheet for the Friday afternoon meeting with the executive team, a meeting he would make only if his flight was not late. He had written a few comments on the draft. When Becky returned later, she was shocked to see "Friday" on Peter's note, since she was under a deadline herself and was not aware of his Friday meeting. To make things worse, she was not able to decipher all his comments and was confused about a reference to something he wanted inserted. Peter was forever doing these things to her, so she decided to work on her own project and if there was time left, she would try to figure out what he wanted.

Make no mistake here: The single most important thing we can do to develop high EQ in an employee is to model it ourselves! That is the reason why this book emphasizes self-development. It is a natural human tendency to think that the problem is "out there." *If I could just get them to do the right thing, this department would do just fine.* Employees emulate what we do as managers. We set the tone, and they model our behavior, the good and the bad.

If our own superiors have marginal leadership skills, this does not excuse our own low EQ behavior. We can still have an exemplary department or team by improving our own behavior and working in our own sphere of influence. *You* can do the right things, even if your own boss doesn't. Resolve to faithfully practice what you have learned so far, before you try to change others.

If we are having organizational problems (poor morale, high turnover, low productivity, and poor quality are warning signs!), look inward. When you accept responsibility for the problem, you have considerable control over its resolution. When we make improvements in our own EQ by concentrating on the six facets of self-awareness, self-confidence, self-control, empathy, motivation, and social competency, others will behave more competently. We cannot positively influence others until we have our own house in order. After we become good models ourselves, there are several other steps we can take to develop our employees' EQ.

1. Set Expectations.

Have you ever worked for someone like Peter who is not clear about what is expected of you? It is pretty frustrating, isn't it? We cannot do our best in such circumstances. To develop greater competencies in others, be sure your goals and expectations are very carefully spelled out. Always check the employees' understanding by getting them to explain back to you what they think they're expected to do.

Help your employees set expectations that are challenging but not overwhelming. Goals that are impossibly high and goals that are insultingly low do not motivate us to perform at our best. Discuss and negotiate specific goals and deadlines with your employees and be willing to compromise a little. As employees become more and more competent, some goals can be moved up or broadened in scope on an individual basis.

Be especially cautious about playing favorites — letting certain employees get away with doing less work or breaking rules, or even having the choice assignments. This is a sure-fire way to create resentment! We should expect and demand an equivalent level of performance from everyone, including ourselves, and avoid even the appearance of favoritism if we want to get the most out of everyone, and engender loyalty.

2. Be Accessible and Supportive.

People will work harder for us if they know they can come to us with problems or questions. Make sure everyone knows that you are there for them anytime they need you. If we allow ourselves to become so busy with other things that we are literally never in the office and never available to our staff, we build mistrust and undermine loyalty — hardly the stuff of leadership! Your career will take care of itself if you build it on solid EQ footing, rather than playing politics.

Being accessible is not difficult, if you understand that it involves more than time. When an employee comes to you about something, stop what you are doing and *listen* attentively, or schedule a mutually agreeable time to get together when you can truly listen. Some managers assume that being available and "nice" increases staff dependency. Not so: Increased dependency only occurs when employees have to come to you for every answer, or approval for every step. (See the next section on Empowerment.)

When an employee comes to us with a problem, we need to let them tell their full story. Once they do, we can ask questions. Before we jump in with the answers, we need to ask them what else they can think of to try. Challenge them to stretch; be willing to brainstorm and problem-solve, and suggest where to go for answers or resources.

A climate of openness is a positive thing for any organization, but there will be times when you will not be able to share information about some things. If you truly cannot tell your employees something, tell them that you are not yet able to share it, but you will do so as soon as you can. Do not give the impression that you are distancing yourself from the team because that will result in rumor and even distrust. Effective leadership, like most productive efforts, is a balancing act.

3. Empower Your Employees.

Employees will indeed come to us with problems, especially if we maintain an open-door policy. But simply providing all the answers and sending them on their way will not help develop their potential to solve such problems in the future. If we want employees to begin taking on more responsibility, we must help them by *not* giving them answers but, instead, by asking them questions so they can come up with the answers on their own. We should then earnestly compliment them for figuring out the answer themselves, and encourage them to go through the same steps the next time.

Employees will step forward and take on responsibility if the risk of repercussion is removed. If we expect empowered behavior, we must be willing to stand behind people when they make a decision. If they use good judgment and act reasonably based on the facts, back them up, even if the outcome is less than satisfactory. People are afraid to take risk when they believe they will be punished for failure. Instead of a reprimand, it's far more effective to say:

> *"It doesn't look like that turned out well, June. Let's see if we can figure out what went wrong and how we can prevent it next time."*

Employees will learn from their mistakes when we help them, and they will virtually never make those same mistakes again! This approach will not demoralize or squelch enthusiasm for the job, either; instead it will encourage them to take responsibility and show that we respect their judgment.

4. Provide Frequent and Positive Feedback.

Providing frequent and positive feedback is one of the most fundamental ways of developing others. Most people receive far too little feedback from their managers, good or bad, yet we know that everyone (managers included) works harder at the things they are encouraged to do. Social rewards such as compliments and thank you's are strong incentives, as strange as that seems. Most employees are not accustomed to receiving praise, so our approval can be particularly rewarding.

Behavior that is reinforced will increase, but we need to know what to reinforce. Stay in close contact with your employees so you will know when they are doing things well. If you are not sure what people are doing, ask individual workers to bring you up to date on their work.

One good suggestion is to make a plan to periodically tell employees what they are doing that *is good*. Compliment them in writing, face-to-face, and electronically. Recognize them in front of peers at staff meetings. Be creative, but whatever you do, make it your business to *look for things the staff is doing well*. This gives them an incentive to keep working even harder at those things they are complimented about, and to keep up or increase this level of performance. The more praise you give, the less reason for correction, because minor problem behaviors begin to take care of themselves. As people do more of what's right, they will have less time to do things wrong.

Suggestions for Using Feedback to Develop an Employee

The following exercise is an excellent way to integrate the information from this chapter. Put it to work by using feedback with your own department or team:

1. Pick your weakest employee and think of one thing he or she does well, and look for areas of similarity or areas where the two of you agree.

2. Write a *Walk-in-Their-Shoes* (EQ Fundamentals) paragraph where you imagine what he or she is thinking and feeling to try to gain some additional understanding of his or her perspective.

3. Go to that person and genuinely compliment him or her on one thing he or she has recently done well, and tell him or her what you appreciate about him or her.

4. At least twice a week for a month, compliment the employee on something he or she has done well. Establish a climate of trust and acceptance.

Suggestions for Using Feedback to Develop an Employee

5. At the end of the month, evaluate the employee's recent performance or attitude. The performance is very likely to have improved, just because you related a little differently to him or her. If it has, tell the employee that you are seeing improvement in his or her performance and that you appreciate their hard work. If it has not improved, continue the compliments and extend an offer to talk to him or her about any problems he or she is experiencing. Spend more time with the employee, including coaching on how to improve. If attitude and performance do not improve in three months, it's time to transfer the employee to a department where he or she would be happier, or else terminate the employee. (This is explored further in the Positive Confrontations section that follows.)

6. When you have managed to turn around your weakest employee, do the same with your next-lowest employee.

Remember: Don't abruptly stop the compliments. In fact, continue praising all employees, not just the weak ones. Show appreciation to everyone by continuing to look for things each employee is doing right, and tell them what you are noticing.

5. Help Employees Maintain Emotional Balance.

The workplace itself can be stressful, but workers often bring their problems to the job. A good manager must not be uncomfortable when an employee comes in extremely upset, angry, or worried. As we have learned, emotions in the office are normal and helpful in guiding our action. Good managers need to tune in to what their employees are feeling and help them regain self-control and act appropriately. Their followers will respect them for it.

Suggestions for Helping an Employee Deal with Anger

Intense anger is particularly challenging in the office. If the imminent safety of you or anyone else is in jeopardy, follow the security procedures set up for such occasions. The following suggestions are appropriate for most situations:

1. Get the angry person's attention and offer to talk one-to-one.

2. Use your best listening skills to hear the person out. Just being able to vent with somebody who cares might take care of most of the problem, leaving you with little you need to say or do.

3. Empathize with the employee's concerns (remind yourself that empathy is not the same as agreement).

4. Use *"Process" Comments* (see Fundamentals) to help uncover what's really happening. ("What's really going on here between you two?")

5. Make some suggestions for what he or she can do to positively deal with anger (see Chapter 7).

6. Offer to problem-solve with the person, helping him or her to think of options.

7. Encourage the employee to take time to calm down — perhaps even work on something else for awhile.

Positive Confrontations

Even the best performers occasionally need correction, constructive criticism, or refocusing. Confrontation itself is a touchy issue for many managers, and we tend to put it off until the problem is really out of hand. At this point, we are likely to become angry ourselves and more likely to be overly critical. However, harsh and demoralizing criticism is *not* the mark of an emotionally intelligent leader. We must remember the purpose of a criticism: to help the employee grow and improve, rather than to punish someone.

Emotionally intelligent leaders know that issuing criticism can be an important opportunity for growth, if it's done with the right intentions. They enter into any such confrontation determined to make it a dialog and to help the employee grow and learn. Receiving criticism can be emotionally upsetting to many employees; be sensitive to what they're feeling and do not be critical of the person — just the offending behavior.

A good critique focuses on the problem and seeks out the employee's side of the story. Let them share it from their perspective. Turn it into an opportunity to problem-solve as you both work on ideas for improvement. All confrontations should be delivered face-to-face and in private, and include our best listening and empathy skills. Discussing any problem when it first appears, before it becomes an ingrained habit, is an important key.

Suggestions for Positive Confrontations

1. Before the confrontation, try to describe the situation from the employee's perspective in your mind or on paper. (See *Walk in Their Shoes* in the Fundamentals section in Chapter 4.)

2. State the problem that you observed (or heard) by simply giving factual information and using "I" messages, without making an accusation or evaluation. ("Pete, that report had a lot of errors, and I was disappointed in your performance" instead of "Pete, you blew it again. How could you even think we would send that lousy work to corporate?")

3. Ask for the other person's explanation, reason, or side of the story ("What happened?" or "Tell me your side of things."). Perhaps he or she has a point or you missed something. Allow for that possibility.

4. If you are still convinced that the behavior or performance is unacceptable, patiently explain why. Reiterate your expectations and the talents and abilities he or she has to meet those standards ("You're one of the best analysts I have, and you are capable of better. I want this report to include...").

Suggestions for Positive Confrontations

5. Use a *"Process" Comment* (Fundamentals) to focus on the "how" of the work, rather than merely the contents or results.

6. If the employee becomes emotional and shows anger, hurt, or embarrassment, empathize with him or her. Do not back away from these feelings — encourage the employee to express them.

7. Problem-solve with the employee ("What can we do to be sure this doesn't happen again?" or "What can we do to correct this situation, now that it has occurred?"). Encourage him or her to offer at least one idea, and avoid giving the answers yourself.

8. Mutually agree on what is to be done, and express your confidence in his or her ability to carry out the plan.

CHAPTER 12

Putting EQ to Work: The Team

Sharon proceeded to the conference room with a feeling of dread. She called a team meeting for this afternoon only because she had been told to do so. She preferred to relate to her team members individually or by e-mail, rather than get the group together in the same room. This time, they all needed to be told at the same time about their new reporting relationships under the partial restructuring. Sharon was well aware that whenever their team was together, Tom and Sarah were always at each other's throats, leaving the others feeling mostly disgusted or bored. Today's discussion promised to be especially difficult. Sharon knew she should be able to control them, but this "group" she had inherited six months ago was a team in name only, and she felt discouraged about anything positive coming out of the afternoon.

Teams and other small groups are now the mainstays of many organizations, and leaders are increasingly called upon to work with groups of people collectively. Skills for leading the group are built upon the individual relationships we establish with each team member, and teams call for many of the same relationship behaviors. In addition to building relationships with each individual member of the team, there are certain team skills that good leaders put to use in order to build the Emotional Intelligence of the team and promote good relationships.

The Leader's Role with Teams

In high-functioning team structures, the role of the leader becomes one of coach or facilitator. As leaders, we need to be certain that we have the necessary breadth of skills present within the team to accomplish the goals — a healthy diversity of skills and ideas that we refer to from time to time so members appreciate individual strengths and help keep them in balance within the team dynamic.

We must be sure we can help the team obtain the resources it needs to do its job. Help them establish goals and obtain what they need, and then get out of their way and let them work! It's not necessary or advisable to look over their shoulders as they work; just remain available for problem-solving, if necessary. Continue to offer them encouragement and support, but hold them accountable for results. And, like a good coach, when they make a mistake, be sure to help them figure out what went wrong before you send them back into the game.

Using Participation and Empowerment

High EQ leaders make the most of all the talents at their disposal but avoid the mistaken notion that they are expected to have all the answers. Emotionally intelligent leaders know that a high-functioning team can almost always come up with better answers than any one person, themselves included.

In order for the team to help us, we must be willing to give them as much information as possible. Keep them informed about the good news and the bad news: This will build trust and ensure that they will pitch in in a crisis. If we expect employees to operate like a team, we must include them in decision-making and keep them informed about their progress as a group, how the group's work fits with the organization's goals, and about decisions made by upper management. If things are looking bleak, the rumor mill always operates anyway, so give them the truth.

The team also needs to know why a change is necessary. If they are operating on the assumption that things are going well because they have not been informed of the dwindling market share or declining profits, team members will see no need for any change and will resist it when change is introduced. Employees are much less resistant to change and will, in fact, embrace needed change if they understand the problem or need and if they have been part of developing a solution to meet that need.

To put this on a practical level, let's say that you have been asked to cut the department's budget by 5%. One way to do this is to make the decisions yourself as to what to cut. A far more effective, high-EQ way to handle this is to go to the team and say, "This is the situation we are facing. Give me your ideas on what we can do to streamline our budget." Some intense emotions will surface, but the leader with high EQ will use his or her sense of empathy and genuine caring to let people channel their emotions by expressing them. Only then can the team move beyond anger and worry and work together, brainstorming solutions. Solving problems as a group will help channel their energy and almost always result in a far better plan than the manager could have developed alone.

Never underestimate the importance of buy-in. Employees will cooperate and try to make the changes work out when they have been part of creating those changes, particularly when you share information with them that helps them understand why tough choices and sacrifices are necessary. Participation builds self-confidence, loyalty, and motivation. It empowers people when they are part of a solution. If you do not allow them to participate in shaping their future in good times as well as bad, resistance to change will be greater and you will notice more anger, less motivation, lower productivity, and generally low EQ behavior.

One Dominant Team Member

Teams often include one very verbal team member who always knows the answers, and who tends to rush headlong into action. This can be very frustrating for the rest of the team, but the real danger in allowing one or two people to dominate the team is that it tends to intimidate and inhibit others. Quieter members might give up and become less involved, letting their more aggressive peers take over. Others will become very resentful. This must not escape your notice; it can be handled individually and within the team setting.

Suggestions for Involving All Team Members

1. Talk to the dominant person or persons individually and coach them on how to hold back and let others speak first "so others can learn, too."

2. Give them extra projects or responsibilities that will tap their enthusiasm. Ask for their help with something specific.

3. In the meetings, thank the dominant person for his or her comments before he or she gets too far into them, and ask the more reserved members, by name, for their opinions. If you repeat this pattern several times, the interaction will probably become more balanced.

4. We can also use *"Process" Comments* (EQ Fundamentals) ("Paul is the only one speaking up here, and I'm not hearing anything from the rest of you. What's happening with the team?").

Be alert to possible conflict, which brings us to our next topic.

Dealing with Team Conflict

Team conflict, as a rule, is normal and acceptable. Some kinds of conflict help us arrive at better solutions to problems, and the very act of working through conflict to the resolution phase builds team cohesiveness. In fact, the presence of some conflict indicates that there is energy around a certain issue. The team is motivated — they are just not all moving in the same direction. Conflict only becomes problematic when neither the leader nor the team understands how to redirect that energy so that the entire team is moving together in the same direction.

Avoid the tendency to take over. When conflict arises in the team, some managers simply make a decision themselves and cast the tie-breaking vote. This looks like the best route for the short-term, but they need to realize that unresolved conflict will come back in other, sometimes more virulent, forms. The leader with high Emotional Intelligence knows that you have to balance conflicting perspectives to get the best results and preserve unity. When conflict arises in the group, accept it; take a deep breath, and deal with it calmly. As leaders, we must remain neutral, at least initially, in order to empower the team.

Suggestions for Resolving Team Conflict

1. Begin by briefly summarizing the two conflicting perspectives as you see them.

2. Use the *"Three-Step"* from Fundamentals to prepare and follow the group conflict revision, below:

   - Explain the rules: *Each side will take turns. The speaker is absolutely not to be interrupted, and everyone will listen calmly and quietly.* Ask for a volunteer from each side to provide everyone with more information. When they present their side, ask someone with an opposing or neutral viewpoint to summarize what the speaker said (they will probably be summarizing a perspective different from their own). Do *not* allow the argument to resume, but focus on one side only.

   - Allow the other side equal time and equal respect as another speaker tells their viewpoint or advances their reasoning. Again, have someone who is neutral or who holds a different view summarize their point of view.

   - Begin problem solving. Ask the team if anyone sees any points of agreement, and try to offer some points of agreement yourself. Say something that bridges the gap, even if all you can think of is, "Well, I know you are both trying to do what you think is most in line with our goals." Open the floor to everyone for ideas. Rather than asking for opinions and doing a majority vote, however, think in terms of "How many possible ways can we think of to resolve this problem?" Get someone to record these ideas in front of the group on a whiteboard or flipchart.

Suggestions for Resolving Team Conflict

3. Avoid latching onto a simple compromise. Encourage the group to think of creative solutions or of things that incorporate certain features of both perspectives. Try to think in terms of adding elements to the solution, rather than taking things away from either side.

4. Adopt the plan that seems most reasonable to the group as a whole. If there is still no agreement, ask people to think about the issue overnight and come back tomorrow ready to make the decision, or tell them you will have to make it yourself.

5. Do not allow tempers to flare up. Never tolerate name-calling or disrespect for any team member. Be sure that you remain in control of yourself.

6. If the conflict is deep-seated or highly divisive, bring in an outside mediator who is trained in conflict resolution. Observe this person carefully so that you can emulate some of the same behaviors next time.

If you deal positively with conflict, the team will have more self-control and more motivation as members work to solve problems *together* under an able leader. Working through conflict builds team trust and cohesiveness, and greatly increases team EQ.

Dealing with Personality Conflicts

Good leaders maintain an attitude of *no tolerance for intolerance*. Racial, religious, gender, or any other kind of hatred has no place in the workplace. Hatred is devastating to performance and must be confronted immediately. Even in a fairly tolerant department where these issues are not divisive, there will be personality conflicts. Deal with them only if they become disruptive to the team as a whole or interrupt work flow. Encourage each party to talk privately to the other. If they are hesitant to do so, offer to be the neutral party. You might find the suggestions for resolving team conflict helpful, in addition to those that follow.

Suggestions for Dealing with Personality Conflicts

1. If you talk to each party individually, help them reframe. Challenge the assumptions that underlie the conflict.

2. Arrange to meet with both people together. Explain that you are all getting together to work out differences and improve team relationships. The parties should sit face-to-face and talk to each other — not to you.

3. Use the *"Three-Step"* method of conflict resolution. (See Fundamentals.)

4. Ask all sides to shake hands; praise them for their hard work and cooperation.

5. Compliment each of them, mentioning something you appreciate about each.

6. Make a *"Process" Comment* about how things went in the discussion. See details in EQ Fundamentals.

7. If you think it is necessary, have someone type up what has been agreed to, ask for their signatures, and place a copy in the file for future reference.

Conclusion

Our Emotional Intelligence can be used to lead others, but it will take practice. EQ skills are extremely effective, and we can *all* master them. But first we must *want* to improve! Emotions are present in every aspect of our daily lives. The ways we use them will help determine career success and affect all our relationships. It is critical that we learn to develop self-awareness, self-confidence, self-control, empathy, motivation, and social competency — and use them wisely.

Take a few minutes to review the three goals you set in Chapter 3, based on the Self-Assessment and Leadership-Assessment Checklists.

What have you learned about how to improve these areas? How can you continue working on them? Remember: This is a long-term process; substantial improvement will not be evident for at least six months. But if you fail to try to put these principles into practice, where will you be in six months? Probably right where you are now, if not in an even worse position.

What three long-term changes are you willing to make, based on what you have learned about yourself and how you can improve your Emotional Intelligence? Write these below:

1) _____

2) _____

3) _____

If you use your emotional brain to balance your rational brain, you cannot be stopped. Do not let the presence of emotions in the workplace scare you. Instead, harness their energy for improved interpersonal relationships and increased productivity.

Now, go for it!

About the Author. . .

Emily A. Sterrett is President of her own training and management consulting firm, PerformanceWorks, LLC. She has over twenty years' experience in project and people management, career counseling, and college teaching in management and psychology. She has a Ph.D. in Social Psychology and is a Licensed Professional Counselor. Her consulting specialties include leadership development, emotional intelligence, teambuilding, and employee morale and retention. The concept of EQ integrates many of the ideas she believes in passionately and that have worked with her many satisfied OD clients. Her other publication, *Leadership Foundations* (available from Virginia Philpott Manufacturing Extension Partnership), a practical guide for frontline leaders, has been highly acclaimed.